"The Millennial Money Fix by Douglas and Heather Boneparth provides a fiscal roadmap for today's largest generation, Millennials. The book offers multiple lessons in financial literacy, which will be eye-opening for some readers but are necessary for all young people to know."

—Leah Ingram, author,
The Complete Guide to Paying for College

"The Millennial Money Fix highlights two of today's concerns, the higher education bubble and the changing job market. Douglas and Heather Boneparth accurately describe the higher education bubble and the coming changes in the job market in a pragmatic way most people haven't read. The Boneparths then give their readers reliable solutions to address these problems and, ultimately, achieve financial freedom."

—Debt Free Guys, money bloggers and authors,
4: The Four Principles of a Debt Free Life

THE
MILLENNIAL
MONEY FIX

What You Need to Know About
Budgeting, **Debt**, and **Finding**
Financial Freedom

Douglas A. Boneparth, CFP®, MBA
and Heather J. Boneparth, Esq.

CAREER
PRESS

Wayne, N.J.

THE MILLENIAL MONEY FIX
EDITED BY ROGER SHEETY
TYPESET BY KARA KUMPEL
Cover design by Jonathan Bush Design
Benjamin Franklin image by Galushko Sergey/shutterstock
Printed in the U.S.A.

To order this title, please call toll-free 1-800-CAREER-1 (NJ and Canada: 201-848-0310) to order using VISA or MasterCard, or for further information on books from Career Press.

The Career Press, Inc.
12 Parish Drive
Wayne, NJ 07470
www.careerpress.com

Library of Congress Cataloging-in-Publication Data

CIP Data Available Upon Request.

To Hazel, our Greatest Thing in Life.

CONTENTS

CHAPTER ONE

THE MILLENNIAL PROBLEM

The year was 2003, a time when 50 Cent and the Ying Yang Twins ruled the Billboard charts. The place was Gainesville, Florida, a town where college dreams are made. Well, mine were at least. I showed up early to take summer classes and get a taste of independence. It was absolutely amazing. I could do whatever I wanted—assuming I made passing grades and didn't get arrested. My first act of freedom brought me to the tattoo shop downtown, where I paid actual money to have a silver loop stapled into my left eyebrow. Rebellious, right? In all fairness, face jewels were marginally cool back then. And I ripped the thing out after just four days, when it started to itch.

Independence is one hell of a drug.

My four years at Florida were a dream, so great at times they did not seem real. Raised to have what our parents would call a "good head on my shoulders," I was a good boy. I made good (enough) decisions, which led to my first hints of the Great Things in Life. I witnessed three national championships from the Gator football and basketball teams, made lifelong friends through my fraternity, received an early start on the career I love, and—most important of all— met my wife, Heather. It all plays back in my head like a slow montage to the tune of "(I've Had) The Time of My Life." *Sigh.*

But as the eyebrow ring suggested, I was also a bit young and stupid. Even with a financial advisor as a father and an internship working in his practice, I was not mature enough to make the right decisions all the time. For one, I dropped out of the business school to pursue an easier degree in public relations, just because I didn't feel like taking financial accounting. I heard it was hard. I borrowed student loans from a private lender for my rather small tuition payments. (Why didn't Dad stop me? I don't know.) And I dumped a disproportionate amount of cash into spiffing up and tricking out my 2004 Subaru Impreza WRX. It's startling how much money a cat-less exhaust system, sport springs, an STI bookshelf spoiler, 17-inch gunmetal Prodrive 10-spoke rims, painted side skirts, and a custom front mesh grill could cost. Not to mention my weekly trips to the local "dent specialist" at 20 bucks a pop. The Campus Lodge parking lot was treacherous for my baby.

In a sense, each one of these gaffes stemmed from my lack of financial literacy, and with some basic calculations, I could have done better. Even when my choices were poor judgment calls rather than outright mistakes, if I had been equipped with more knowledge, maybe I would have chosen better. And my decisions had little consequences. Others—including Heather's—could affect the rest of your life.

WE ARE FINANCIALLY ILLITERATE

The financial issues of all living generations are cut from the same bedrock: a lack of financial literacy. When asked questions about their retirement in a 2014 survey by The American College of Financial Services, only 20 percent of retirement-age adults received a passing score.[1] These people are about to *retire*. They can't afford to make new mistakes, let alone pass them down to their children (us). The Financial Industry Regulatory Authority (FINRA) asked 25,000 Americans of all ages five questions covering everyday concepts like compound interest and inflation. Sixty-three percent got three or less correct.[2]

There's more statistics to go around, but you get the gist: no age group knows it all when it comes to financial wellness. We could all use some work. Hell, if my dad was not a financial advisor who engrained personal finance in my brain, I would be just as bad.

Put aside the coursework I took to become a financial advisor myself and not a single class in two decades of schooling would have provided me the tools to make informed financial decisions. I never received a proper lesson on cash flow, debt management, credit, or investments. And without understanding these topics, we only learn lessons by reacting to our lives' choppy waters—correcting the mistakes that we've already made.

Without question, Millennials need to learn even more because our financial landscapes are more complicated today than those of our parents and theirs. In fact, we may be even less knowledgeable than our elders because coming of age this century hasn't required the same level of vigilance to assure our survival.

Or maybe that's just what we assumed.

The Greatest Generation was great for a reason. They worked incredibly hard so their children and grandchildren could live better lives. Many were immigrants, escaping religious, political, and ethnic persecution. As if that wasn't enough, they lived through the Great Depression. They overcame historical obstacles and made the kinds of sacrifices I hope we never have to. I admire their legacy—including that of my grandfather, a true World War II hero—more than words can state here. But these difficult experiences shaped their financial behaviors. I used to joke about my grandparents hiding money under their mattresses, but the fear wasn't funny to them.

When it came to managing their finances, their caution cut both ways. Their well-founded worry that everything could be taken away from them in an instant drove them toward prudent decision-making skills. The mantra was that you didn't spend more than you had, and if you had to borrow, you paid it back as soon as you could. They had a healthy dose of skepticism, but you can't blame them, given what they had witnessed.

At the same time, fear from their experiences may have limited how far some members of the Greatest Generation felt they could reach. But pairing a relatively less complex economy with their cautious approach to personal finance helped them build conservative and stable lives for their families.

They gave birth to the Baby Boomers, or as I see them, our parents. Mom and Dad were more optimistic than their parents, perhaps too much so. Like our grandparents, they were not immune to the effects of conflict. For many, the Vietnam War sent childhood friends to fight for "freedom" once again, and the Cold War reminded everyone that technology could be as terrifying as it could be exciting. The Civil Rights Movement further fanned the flames during an already tumultuous time.

Despite these obstacles, Baby Boomers had greater advantages. They found promising new opportunities by acquiring a finer set of skills from going to college and earning advanced degrees. They could apply their unprecedented access to information and education on top of the foundation their parents laid for them.

Our parents welcomed freer thinking. Armed with advanced degrees, they could afford to do things such as improve the family franchise, venture into cutting-edge industries, or be bold enough to embark on new business ideas that were once considered impractical. But in doing so, they distanced themselves from that cautious financial mindset.

Some Boomers couldn't acquire the financial knowledge needed to keep up with an increasingly complex economy muddled by slippery new financial products. Although their willingness to experiment, carry a bolder attitude, and assume new risks expanded what was possible, Boomers, like their parents, still lacked that basic financial training. It would only be a matter of time before it caught up with them. By 2008, we all saw how over-levered people created, and fell victim to, the worst financial landscape since the Depression decades earlier.

Yes, I mean the housing crisis. So many people assumed mortgages they couldn't afford and treated their homes like endless pits of money. Of course, banks as predatory lenders should not have been offering those terms in the first place. But I wonder: would people equipped with more financial knowledge have accepted terms to loans that seemed too good to be true? Would they have overextended themselves using the place that keeps them warm at night? Maybe a more informed public could have prevented such a major economic mess. I'm aware that it's not that simple, but this much is true: a financially literate person makes more informed decisions.

Now this timeless issue has caught up with Millennials in the same way. Like our parents had over their parents, we have more advantages from our greater access to information, education, and technology. In a more peaceful America, our life experiences have been colored by far less adversity and conflict. But even if we experienced better childhoods, it took us one step further away from the lessons learned by our grandparents and even our great-grandparents.

Our cautions eroded, we've grown into ill-equipped young adults who are not ready to tackle the outrageous cost of the higher education we need to thrive. After graduating with unprecedented student loan debt, today's unchartered labor environment then challenges our ability to jumpstart meaningful careers and our adult lives. This is the very essence of the Millennial Problem. It's ugly and the obstacles we face are uniquely ours.

We can't look to our parents for answers—they've got their own issues. They can't make it all better, like we're living some bad childhood nightmare. What does this mean in real-world terms? It means that when your parents put money into your bank accounts on an as-needed basis, it can temporarily help but will not solve your problem. Bailouts of any kind, whether from Uncle Sam or your rich Uncle Steve, do not solve anything unless they're coupled with the education to avoid needing those bailouts again. To quote Fat Bastard from the acclaimed *Austin Powers* trilogy, "It's a vicious cycle!"

When categorizing the moving elements of our lives, the most crucial are health, family, time, and money. They can be weighted in this order. Without your health, you can't care for your family, or acquire and spend your wealth. Family or loved ones are a close second. They drive you to achieve, relish in your success, and satisfy your heart. Time is something we can't get back, and finding ways to maximize it allows for a more fulfilling life. Money can't be left off this list because it facilitates your ability to experience great material and immaterial things.

We are taught as children about the first three of these things. How to: (1) physically take care of ourselves; (2) share love with others; and (3) manage our time. Why are we not taught the final missing piece?

Financial literacy works to eliminate the phrase, "if only I knew then what I know now." It's a mission to provide financial knowledge and equip people with the information they need to be proactive instead of reactive. Being reactive makes people vulnerable to mistakes that they could end up paying for (or repaying) for the rest of their lives. It sets you up to inevitably fail somewhere down the line, or right at the starting line.

I don't know about you, but failure has never been an option for me.

Schools have the best platform to start teaching young people about financial and economic issues, and they're just not working fast enough. The Council for Economic Education's 2016 Survey of the States showed that we weren't doing any better in bringing these concepts into the classroom in 2016 than in 2014. Only 20 states require high school students to take an economics course (up two from 2014), and only 17 states require them to take a course in personal finance (the same as 2014). And despite the rising spotlight on financial literacy, only two more states have added personal finance into their required K–12 standards.[3] Age-appropriate coursework in grade school would be the most ideal place to start financial education because it captures young people's attention in a setting they are comfortable with, and presents the opportunity for kids to bring the dialogue home to their parents, encouraging a healthier financial lifestyle for the whole family.

But we Millennials weren't healthy as kids. We ate Taco Bell and all-you-can-eat pizza at Cicis; not organic produce and conversations about personal finance. We were devoid of all nutrition. I'd argue that even if one course on personal finance nudged its way into our high school curriculum, it would not have resonated enough to change things for our generation. Financial literacy isn't gauged by how you answer one set of multiple-choice questions. It's a litmus test on how ready you are to handle critical financial decisions as they arise in your life.

Older Millennials faced some of those decisions already, and many decided wrong. As you read this book, you may find yourself saying those infamous words, "if I only knew then what I know now." And that's okay.

Because as you learn, you'll be gaining the skills to never say it again.

OUR $1.3 TRILLION BUBBLE

Imagine shopping for a new mattress at one of those mattress showroom stores. You know, one where the guy walks around in an oversized Joseph A. Bank suit, trying to sell you on the queen deluxe pillow topper with a hypoallergenic coating. You planned to buy a cheaper mattress and pay for the whole thing upfront. But the guy offers some pretty sexy financing on the deluxe option—zero percent down and zero percent interest for one year. You stand at the register rationalizing the decision: "Man, it would be awesome to avoid paying for this sweet mattress right now. I can get the 72-inch flat screen of my dreams *today!*"

But two years pass, not one. Now, a mattress that you could have purchased in full (had you not chosen the fancy pillow top) or you could have paid off faster (had you not sprung for the 72-inch flat screen) will cost you even more due to an exorbitant interest rate. Did you make the wrong choice? Probably, but only hindsight tells you that. Now, you're stuck with a good that cost you more than it could have. That mattress store and its bank placed a bet against you, and they won.

Colleges are not mattress stores. Indeed, paying for college with student loans is not the same as buying goods that depreciate in value. The knowledge you gain from pursuing a college degree makes *you* appreciate in value. Without a doubt, educated people make our society better. But why are we financing our education the same way as mattresses? It feels like people placed similar bets against Millennials, hoping we wouldn't win. And the stakes are higher than ever before.

The nation's student loan debt has grown to more than $1.3 trillion. Truly, it took an entire generation to amass that many zeros. The average debt per college student in the Class of 2016 is $37,172, which reflects an increase of 6 percent per student from 2015.[4] The trend is disturbing, considering that in a decade, the average debt at graduation rose at more than *twice* the rate of inflation.[5] There are now more than 44 million student borrowers in this country, 90-something percent more than even 10 years ago.[6]

Most troubling is when people don't repay it. The delinquency rate for federal student loans stands at 11.3 percent of borrowers. In case that figure seems rather small to be sounding the alarm, don't be misled, because being "delinquent" is only one way to screw up your repayment. Lend Edu reports that 4.9 million borrowers are in deferment,[7] which allows graduates to temporarily postpone their payments as interest continues to accumulate. It's kind of like putting a Band-Aid on a bullet wound. These delinquent and deferred payments have collectively formed a student loan bubble that's growing larger. And bubbles don't deflate; they burst.

One contributing factor to this problem arose when President George W. Bush signed into law the Grad PLUS Loan Program as part of a deficit-reduction plan. Grad PLUS Loans allow graduate students to borrow up to the "cost of attendance" (as determined by the school) to fund what are often very, very fancy graduate degrees. Students are provided this option with little inquiry into whether they can repay the amounts borrowed. Often, graduate students borrow Grad PLUS Loans after they've hit their ceiling on Stafford Loans, a primary source of college funding, which we will discuss in detail later.

The reason Grad PLUS Loans are so significant is because the money borrowed by graduate students makes up nearly 40 percent of the entire $1.3 trillion loan portfolio, even though the graduate students themselves only represent 16 percent of all student borrowers.[8]

Why would the federal government give any student such sky-high access to borrowing? Is a 20-something-year-old recent college grad that much more equipped to make the better financial decisions than an 18-year-old rising college freshman? I refuse to think so.

So, why then? Try looking at the cost of these graduate programs. Some prestigious private institutions charge the amount of a mortgage for advanced graduate degrees. The only reason they can keep raising tuition costs is because Grad PLUS Loans are available to pay up to the "cost of attendance," as the school determines. Make the money available and students will spend it, plus interest. They are placing the bet.

Graduate student debt is just the extreme end of the student loan scale, which is tipping in the wrong direction. For all student loans, devastating results can occur when you don't analyze the risks and then borrow them in a careless manner. In collegiate terms:

financial illiteracy: student loans :: burning match: gasoline

Both are dangerous combinations.

This isn't the first recent instance of Americans falling victim to their own poor financial decisions involving loans. In 2008, we also saw how bad our behavior can be when borrowing mingles with ignorance about the consequences of incurring debt. The housing crisis looked eerily like what's happening with higher education: the private lender is now the government, whereas the white picket fence is a degree.

Student loans—like all loans—are just a tool. Tools can be very helpful when you know how to use them. But debt is a burden, often insurmountable. The cost of education is out of control and, therefore, student loans are here to stay until affordability becomes an honest priority of our government and institutions. In the meantime, these loans will continue to be sold as free money, enabling students to collect on their "right" to be educated however, and wherever, they desire.

Until students reach graduation day, when all bets are off.

A REROUTED LABOR ENVIRONMENT

There was a time when only the privileged went to college. Only those select few could afford to philosophize while everyone else learned firsthand about the world. Around the age you would graduate from high school, many of our elders faced futures that involved some element of conflict. World War II, the Vietnam War, and the Cold War focused the American people's efforts for decades. Those who were drafted fought, especially during World War II, and many who stayed stateside supported soldiers on the battlefield through their professional work. They welded metal for bombers and filled factory molds for ammunition. Even less technical jobs such as selling war bonds involved learning a trade that fed a wartime demand.

In those times, much of American industry—and our economy as we knew it—revolved around our battles. Patriotism swelled as people did their part, recognizing that their sacrifices or commitments could be part of our country's greater good.

During those times, people widely accepted that college, especially at four-year private institutions, was not for everyone. Vocational work (using your hands) carried great value. But with relative peace came a change. Technical skills decreased in demand, whereas theoretical skills increased due to advancements in technology, medicine, and science.

To further advance the progress being made in these areas, and to combat technical jobs being off-shored to other parts of the world, Generations X and Y had to adapt. Colleges and universities offered the advanced training needed, and more high school graduates felt compelled to attend so they could compete in the modernized world. As more people sought to enroll, more programs emerged to satisfy the need.

The rest is history.

From the late 1980s through the 90s, a major shift in the labor environment was started. Investments in technology swelled, bringing computers into the professional lives of nearly one-half of American workers. Leading up to the infamous Y2K scare, the presence of computers in the workforce grew to make up one-fifth of businesses' new capital investment. In turn, these businesses demanded more advanced skills from their workers, many of whom had specialized college degrees and were equipped to provide those skills in exchange for higher salaries. The competition was on.[9]

By the turn of the century, Americans were only starting to feel the change in their homes and daily lives. Most could not imagine the profound effect that it would have on their jobs. Better technology led to more efficient ways of doing things, and this allowed businesses to complete simple-skill tasks at a much lower cost. Between 1997 and 2012, the labor environment moved significantly away from manufacturing jobs, reducing this once-predominant domestic workforce by around 5.5 million.[10] Technology was starting to make the world a simpler place.

It also bred new ways of doing business altogether, with the rise of e-commerce through online marketplaces such as eBay. Now, you could literally run a business from behind a computer. You could get rich in your pajamas.

As a hobby and then our first business venture, my brother and I spent our spare time fixing computers for people around town. I was raised in Boca Raton, a country club town in South Florida where people move to *end* rather than to *begin*, if you get what I'm saying. The senior citizens needed simple solutions to non-problems, like hitting the escape key or connecting to "the interwebs." My favorite house calls were when wireless routers would go offline. You could tell by the red light glowing and saying, "Stop! No interwebs for you!" To fix them, we'd simply unplug the router and plug it back in. That was the birth of our one-hour minimum policy.

Millennials grew up along with the Internet— it was kind of like an older, much smarter sibling. We were spellbound by clicking through Microsoft Encarta and spending hours dialing up to AOL during peak times (it was *always* busy). Heather once told me she built her own GeoCities Website, filled with shout-outs to her friends and one image of a giant Nike sneaker. The Internet was a limitless space of possibility for her tween amusement. I was not quite as youthful about it, but still had no idea what it would become.

When I graduated college in 2007, the economy still appeared to be thriving in our eyes. Few worried about post-graduate employment because we were the ones obtaining the specialized degrees that we thought would meet domestic industry demands. Things looked rosy enough for many of us to extend our academic careers and attend graduate programs right out of college or soon thereafter.

Unfortunately, we weren't the ancient Mayans. We couldn't have foreseen what lurked at the tail end of our first year in the "real world." After just settling into our new careers and programs, we were submerged into the deep-end of an economic cycle, trying not to drown.

Much of what we thought we knew about our respective professions vanished. Layoffs took hold over anyone and everyone. For managers and bosses, 30 years of loyal service resulted in a severance package, a proverbial high-five, and a premature retirement party. Raging holiday parties and plump bonuses vanished into corporate folklore. All the while, entire recruitment classes of Millennials lost their job offers, as firms across all industries actively slashed costs. Despite wanting to feel like special snowflakes, exempt from the chaos surrounding us, we learned a huge life lesson: it wasn't personal. It was just business.

The Great Recession became the Great Accelerator for companies to harness technology to achieve dramatic cost-savings and salvage what they could. Employees scrambled to stay involved and on the payroll, assuming unfamiliar tasks or working extra hours. More people than ever felt expendable until proven otherwise. It was a matter of survival that started an evolution. Many industries felt the change, but here are just two relevant examples.

Let's first look at the rise of new media and its profound effect on traditional print journalism. Leading up to the Great Recession, more outlets were adopting digital platforms anyway, but a colossal change took place when the markets crashed. Along with the physical size of newspapers and magazines, mastheads were sliced in half. According to the American Society of News Editors, the workforce of daily newspapers diminished by almost 20 percent.[11]

New Websites, blogs, and video content emerged alongside the digital content of preexisting print behemoths. This industry shift in how readers consumed their news left storied writers, editors, and photographers with the task of reinventing what the industry meant to them. Young aspiring journalists who could have secured entry-level roles in the past needed to generate their own value by producing original content or being proactive enough to learn new skills that fit today's needs. That is how they could become indispensable. Publications hope to be nimbler by employing less of these folks full-time and offering competitive pay for jobs as needed. Without a doubt, the work isn't as stable. But as more people specialize their skills and have the chance to freelance with more employers, they could enhance their bargaining power and commoditize their abilities in new ways. It appears to be a double-edged sword.

Another great illustration is law. For decades, "Big Law Associate" was the ultimate job for law school graduates. The position coupled high salaries with infinite hours of ministerial, but billable work: document review, legal research, privacy redactions, etc. Firms could charge clients millions for their team's efforts because the model dictated that with expertise came expense, and clients could afford to pay for it. But the country's top 250 law firms skimmed thousands of attorneys from its rosters in 2009 and 2010.[12] And that only represented the attorneys *with* jobs. Entry-level associate class sizes, once robust and an indicator of firm strength, dwindled to modest dozens, as clients refused to fund the expensive grunt work of underlings who were "too green."

Firms needed to find more efficient ways to staff projects and bring better value to their clients. Business technology changed the game. Using e-discovery software, firms could sift through thousands of documents in a fraction of the time as a room full of attorneys could. Without the need to keep as many full-time associates on the payroll to handle these assignments, firms started creating more part-time, flexible staff attorney positions. They could fill these spots on an as-needed basis with less commitment on both ends. This generates revenue and reduces costs by embracing efficiency, rather than continuing with the outdated models of the past. The real question, then, is who wins and loses from this change.

This is why I'm not going to make a case that our generation is worse off than the 50-something career people who lost their pensions and can't afford to send their kids to college anymore (at least not in this chapter). The Boomers are the ultimate victims of the shift in the labor environment because many of them are too expensive and too inexperienced with technology to adapt. Their institutions changed, leaving some of them in the dust.

Millennials never had an institution to begin with. We don't need to *re*invent ourselves to survive—we need to *invent* ourselves to thrive. No templates. No pathways to partner. No roadmaps for our voyages.

We are forced to pioneer our own careers, relying more on ourselves and less on the traditional corporate model. To gain the relevant knowledge in our fields, we start our own businesses and even engage in contract work. And when we do accept full-time positions at firms, we focus on engaging employers that best align with our personal and professional needs. If they end up not offering what we thought they would, we're not afraid to leave.

Contrary to our critics, this is not because Millennials seek the Holy Grail of Jobs, unwilling to settle for anything less than sunshine, roses, and office beanbag chairs. It's because in this labor environment, we know that our careers are curated by us alone—not programmed into a system.

Millennials redefine risk and purpose in how we approach the workforce. Assuming greater risk can be very lucrative with the proper planning and securities in place. Being less burdened by institutional redundancies means our generation can be more creative and even disrupt markets by solving unique problems. We benefit from greater flexibility and work-life balance because we are entrusted with the responsibility to provide service and produce results from anywhere at any time. We understand the technology that drives our industries, and ultimately our careers, so we can always deliver.

Yet, the risks also expose our undeniable challenge. With less institutional backing, we miss out on access to job-related resources, human capital, and instruction. From a mental standpoint, discipline is huge, and some people just don't have enough of it to stay off Reddit all day. With less performance benchmarks in place, harnessing healthy competition between peers (if you have any) can be impossible. There is also the very real, if not the realest problem of needing to hold down a steady income and being able to afford the significant cost of health insurance and other benefits.

Our passion means so much less if it does not translate to real dollars. We need both to bring us closer to financial independence.

THE MILLENNIAL PROBLEM IS EVERYONE'S PROBLEM

Make no mistake, Millennials matter. We are no longer those darn kids, mere children of the rainmakers and game changers. With Baby Boomers entering retirement, we are actually not kids at all. Our actions moving forward have an impact that cannot be ignored, and here's why.

We are vast. There are more than 83 million Millennials in the United States. That's more than one-quarter of the nation's population.

We are diverse. A whopping 44 percent of Millennials are non-white, more than any past generation of Americans.[13]

We are the workforce. In 2015, Millennials became the largest share of the United States workforce at 34 percent.[14]

We (could) spend money. Millennials account for nearly $1.3 trillion in annual spending, and $430 billion of that money is on discretionary, nonessential goods and services.[15]

There comes a time when people begin to strive for the Great Things in Life, or "GTL." No, not "Gym, Tan, Laundry," for Millennials old enough to remember the MTV show *Jersey Shore* (we should all be lucky enough to forget it). I'm repurposing this term for the rest of this book and the rest of your life. It represents achieving many of the wonderful things we seek: owning a home, getting married, starting a family, traveling the world, launching a business, _____ (you fill in the blank). One way or another, our ability to pursue GTL drives the economy. Our inability to do so will destroy it.

The Great Things in Life are linked to the circular relationship of *productivity* (producing goods and services) and *consumption* (spending money on things).

The more we consume, the greater the demand is to produce. The greater the demand is to produce, the more people find jobs producing things. The more people find jobs producing things, the more people consume in the future. And round and round we go.

Plug Millennials into the housing market for a fine example. If Millennials cannot purchase homes because we are paralyzed by crushing student loan debt, then we are hurting a sector of our economy that contributes to nearly one-fifth of everything produced in our country.[16] Taking it one step further, Millennials who cannot afford housing may also feel compelled to delay getting married or having children to put into those homes. A decline in birth rates could negatively affect production, consumption, and the replenishment of the next generation's workforce.

Speaking of the workforce, even the most doubtful Baby Boomers need to consider how we affect their professional and personal lives. We make up a large portion of their talent pool, and recognizing our evolving skills and needs is imperative to the longevity of their businesses. At the same time, if the Millennial workforce does not thrive in the evolving labor environment, Baby Boomers' retirements could suffer, too, because people who currently work are mostly the ones funding Social Security. If we fail, the system will also fail.

In other words, the Millennial Problem is everyone's problem.

So, let's recap it one more time. The bedrock of our problem is a lack of financial literacy. Millennials, like the generations before them, are not armed with the right knowledge to make informed financial decisions. Without integrating personal finance into everyday life from an early age, people will not understand the full consequences of their crucial life decisions, such as financing college or graduate school, until the repayment bills start rolling in.

One thing is certain: the cost of pursuing higher education has ballooned. And financing an education isn't as simple as financing a home. Value, as you will see later, is subjective to each student. You can't ask someone else to evaluate *for you* whether spending the money for a certain degree is worth it. You must have a deeper understanding of the numbers and your own goals to draw the right conclusions. And in some respects, the rapidly evolving labor environment has far outpaced the college education model, harnessing technology to achieve dramatic cost-savings and throwing out the rulebook on what traditional careers look like.

But this is not about feeling sorry, indebted, or lost.

Millennials and their expensive degrees need to be nimbler than ever because the future of this country will turn on our success. From the Baby Boomers hoping for a peaceful retirement, to Generation Z standing to be led into even more uncertain territory, everyone will be affected by what we do. Millennials must accept the huge investment in our education, embrace technology as it affects our workforce, and

above all else, take ownership over our problem—
even if we didn't create it alone—and pursue the
solution.

Time to get started.

CHAPTER TWO

THE FIX STARTS WITH YOU

Without knowing what we want for our lives, we can't tackle each day with purpose. We would just be clocking in our hours, going through the motions, and phoning it in. That may be sufficient for us to survive our time on this planet, but it isn't enough to truly live. Before addressing the more technical areas of personal finance, this chapter will develop your thought process to help you discover what you really want. In other words, you will work on identifying, quantifying, and prioritizing your goals.

I always start my meetings with clients by asking what their goals are. A question that seems so simple is truly the hardest one. Talk about treacherous terrain. I'm not a therapist, but I should consider becoming one just to handle the prickly situations this question gets me into. Sure, some people get excited—maybe they sought me out because they have a goal and need my help to achieve it. But more often than that, people become defensive, tangled, or upset and I end up giving out more tissues than financial advice.

The prerequisite to making good financial decisions is being honest with yourself and with others. Not everyone is prepared for that; they think it's a numbers game. Good financial decisions must be good for the individual, or they're not good at all.

Honesty requires striking a balance between what our emotions tell us and what is realistic. We all have dreams, and many of us are fortunate enough to live in societies where we are free to pursue them. But life is not an Instagram account—you can't just filter away the details.

Every person has circumstances that potentially limit, even dictate, what is possible. Your greatest desire might be to become a finalist on *The Voice*, but your actual voice is more suitable for the shower than Interscope Records. Don't give up your bathroom jam sessions because, sure, they make you feel good inside. But you would not be a responsible person if you quit your job to audition across the country for a reality vocal competition. Deep down, you know this.

Being honest gets even more complicated when you need to communicate your goals with important people like your partner, family, or colleagues. For example, I bet you can guess one of the most controversial goals that many young married couples deal with—no, it's not whether hubby's T-bone steak is cooked to a perfect medium rare (what is this, 1950?!). It's at what point the couple believes they are ready to have children. We will discuss that more in Chapter 7, but the takeaway here is that your goals become more complicated—not less complicated—when you try to fit them in place with anyone else's. Being truthful with yourself and communicative with others will put you on the best track toward achieving them because you won't have to hide from what you want. As we explore ways to embrace challenges that Millennials face at different crossroads in life, I will constantly remind you of how important this is.

REAL TALK: YOUR HONEST GOALS

So, what are your goals?

Stop reading and take 10 minutes to think about what they are. I want you to do so knowing that these next 10 minutes are just to get your gears turning. You don't need to figure them out today, but the sooner you do, the sooner you can put a plan into action. After all, your goals are very serious and personal choices, and they should be given the right amount of consideration.

Ten minutes. Go.

If you had trouble identifying your goals, don't lose your mind. For the purpose of moving forward, I'm hooking you up with some ideas. Having sat down with many young and motivated Millennials, here are their most common goals:

1. Paying off student debt

2. Starting an entrepreneurial business venture

3. Building an emergency fund

4. Paying for a wedding

5. Purchasing a home

6. Starting a family

7. Being financially independent

Hopefully, you can identify with at least one of these common objectives. Now, write down your goals. Really. Go get a piece of paper and pen and write them down, because seeing them in front of you makes them real.

Before moving on, I must address on the record that "making sick bank" is not a goal. Sometimes, I hear young people boast, with ignorance, that making tons of cash is their goal. I tell them they are wrong.

Earning money is a wonderful thing, but without a purpose for earning that money, it's just something you do. Be motivated by the prospect of achieving something you worked hard for and really want because that motivation is truthful and deliberate. The number in your bank account can facilitate and help you reach your goal, but it can't ever be the goal itself.

Got it? Good.

Once your goals are written down, you need to quantify them by *time* and *value*. This makes them measurable.

Let's use an easy example to quantify: throwing a wedding. *Surprise!* Your loving boyfriend or girlfriend has popped the question. According to Heather, it wasn't much of a surprise when I proposed to her on the steps of Lincoln Center in New York City. My own impatience spoiled things the night before, when I not so subtly suggested she get a manicure and wear a nice dress tomorrow. *Whoops.*

Let's say both sets of parents have retirements to worry about. Maybe your parents are also still supporting your degenerate little brother (you might consider buying him a copy of this book). Therefore, you and your fiancé are on your own to pay for the big day.

No big deal. Let's get to work. Quantify the goal by time and value.

First, by time: *When do you want to get married?*

Second, by value: *How much will the wedding cost?*

You decide you cannot possibly wait longer than two years to experience wedded bliss. After researching the price of wedding vendors, you determine you can put it all together for $18,000. With some real-world fourth grade math, you can easily come up with a plan of action: divide $18,000 by 24 months to reach an amount of $750; the amount you must save every month to walk down the aisle.

Do this for every goal you have written down.

As you might have noticed, quantifying goals with fixed prices is rather easy. You divide the value by the time to arrive at what you would need to save each month to reach that goal. However, there are some goals that don't have an explicit price tag. These are often your long-term goals. Financial independence, a concept known to the older folks as retirement, is the best example of our moving target. The goal shifts and develops with time, and your vision of it may change as you age. But nonetheless, you could put a signpost in the ground today and add it to the list with the knowledge its priority and cost will not stay the same.

Having identified and quantified your financial goals, we are two-thirds of the way there. The last piece is prioritizing them.

Goal priority allows you to organize your financial goals so that you can easily select which you should be saving for at that time. It accounts for your first and last dollars of available savings. In other words, assuming you have more than one financial goal, goal priority helps you understand how to allocate your monthly savings. It also shows you how to amend the plan if you are unable to accomplish one or more of the goals within the timeframe you originally set.

Let's assume you, the newly engaged couple (congratulations again), also want to save money to buy a townhome. You've quantified the goal by time and value: you would like to buy in five years, and the place will cost $300,000. With a 20 percent down payment, closing costs, and some money for furnishings and renovations, you calculate that you will need $75,000 to meet this goal. Using that easy math again, you conclude that you need to save $1,250 per month for five years to purchase the townhome, in addition to the $750 per month for two years for the wedding.

Keep in mind this has nothing to do with being able to actually save money to achieve these goals. That's cash management. But at the least, you have successfully put yourself in a position to understand the cost of your goals and decide which are most important to you now.

If you, the glowing power couple (congrats again, seriously I'm so happy for you guys), decide you want that wonderful dream wedding even sooner, and it's way more important to you than owning a townhome in five years, you can consider putting the home savings goal on the back burner for now. Get it? Using this basic exercise, you can evaluate and prioritize any kind of goal, no matter how big or small.

Last of all, I want to reiterate that it's okay for your goals to change. As a matter of fact, they often do. Life is fickle, and as we navigate our way through it, we find ourselves wanting different things at different times. Whatever the catalyst for change is, having already identified some goals puts you in a better position to pivot toward new ones.

Now use that list of goals as your bookmark moving forward. Let your goals remind you, every time you open this book, why you are committing the time to learn.

YOUR PERSONAL FINANCE ARSENAL

The first chapter explained the obstacles facing Millennials today. They are so complicated and risk sidelining our futures if we don't approach them right. And it's hard to look our problems in the face. Hell, if you'd rather be surfing your Netflix queue than absorbing personal finance, I get it. *Stranger Things* is awesome. But now that you understand the reasons, you have a choice: you can wallow in your struggles or you can overcome them.

Our haters love to say we are jaded, impatient, or entitled. Without question, I know they are wrong. We are not the crybabies they paint us out to be; we just don't have the tools to do it better. If we had to wage war for our own financial futures, we'd be going to battle without any weapons. That needs to change if we're going to change. These weapons do more than help you defend yourself—and you don't even have to debate the Second Amendment to use them! They equip you to be proactive in the financial situations we explore in *The Millennial Money Fix,* and to act with the confidence of knowing you are the one in charge.

Consider the key themes of personal finance your weapons. They will help you make the best decisions when faced with life's most important crossroads, which we will cover in the coming chapters. Some themes, such as cash management, are omnipresent, so they come up often. Others, such as estate planning, come up less often and at very specific times.

Okay, enough hype for now. Your key themes of personal finance are as follows:

Cash Management

"It's all about the Benjamins," said the legendary Puff Daddy, and he was right. I am willing to resort to late 90s hip-hop to prove the salient point that cash is king. Above all other lessons and strategies, this will be the mantra you return to the most. Your ability to manage and understand cash dictates just about everything we will discuss throughout this guide. You will need to understand these sub-concepts about cash:

Cash Flow

Cash flow is the amount of money being transferred in and out of your life. Mastering your cash flow is key. To become a master, you need to look at what you are earning and what you are spending like Neo looks at the Matrix: *it's fluid.* At any given time, you must know how much liquid cash you have available in light of your deposits, withdrawals, and payments due. You should be able to quantify your monthly ins and outs, while also keeping the bigger picture in mind. Meaning, you should be able to visualize your cash flow three months in advance, noting any moneymaking opportunities or big-ticket expenses that may be on the horizon.

Understanding your cash flow can help you truly understand your lifestyle and find places to save money. You may think you're living frugally because you skipped your buddy's bachelor party in Vegas last month, but don't pat yourself on the back until you've reviewed the final numbers. You could be living like a Big Baller Boss at home and not even know it.

Cash flow is the first step toward financial freedom. It's the concept upon which all the other concepts are built.

Savings and the Time Value of Money

If you can manage your cash flow, you might acquire some savings, which is the second aspect of cash management. Savings might sound self-explanatory, but to appreciate its significance, you need to understand the time value of money.

Simply put, receiving a dollar today is worth more than receiving that same dollar in the future because if you have a dollar today, you have the opportunity to earn a return on that dollar. You have the chance to put your money to work and have the interest on that money compound with time and be worth more.

Compound interest is a financial mechanism so powerful that Albert Einstein is alleged to have called it the most powerful force in the universe. Now that's genius.

Loans

The last aspect of cash management involves borrowing money, or taking out loans. When used responsibly, loans can help you facilitate major objectives, such as starting a business or—as discussed earlier—financing your education.

But that same "time value of money" concept that can benefit your savings can bite you in the ass with loans. To borrow money today, you often accrue interest as that loan matures. Therefore, that loan will almost always cost you more than the amount you borrowed in the first place. It makes sense, because why would anyone (other than your parents) lend you money with no strings attached?

Loans can be extremely dangerous to people not financially equipped to pay off their debts. This is especially so for Millennials, who often have no choice but to utilize loans to finance their much-needed higher education—degrees that are earned at a supremely high cost.

Insurance

Throughout your life, you are going to face different types of risk. Purchasing insurance is a way to transfer some of that risk to another entity, such as an insurance company, so that you can alleviate the cost of experiencing a loss or damaging occurrence. *The Millennial Money Fix* will focus on a few specific risks facing Millennials and what can be done to mitigate them. We will discuss when and why you need insurance so that you can protect the people and things that are most important to you.

Investments

Everyone loves to talk about investing. I call it the sizzle of personal finance.

The concept is that to grow your wealth with time, you simply cannot stick your cash in a shoebox. There are tools, disciplines, strategies, and theories on investing. I can see why people believe that investments alone will change their lives, but let me fill you in on a hot piece of advice: investments are not any more important than the other themes here. They must work within the context of your financial capabilities and ultimate goals. You need to earn the right to even start investing.

It kills me when people get turned on with stories of self-anointed "day-traders" who made money fast in a few aggressive moves. *Good for you*, I'd say. If you are hoping to obtain a shady investing secret or the next sexy stock from this book, just put it down and slowly walk away. You'll be back someday.

Taxes

I have never met anyone who gets excited about paying their taxes, and I think half of my fraternity brothers are now accountants. No one wants to pay the government more than they should. For the purposes of this guide, I am going to introduce the role that taxes play in your financial life. There's no evading them, because that's illegal, but there are legitimate ways to lessen your tax burden by understanding how the tax system works and positioning yourself strategically from a tax planning perspective.

For many Millennials, taxes are pretty straightforward. However, I want you to have at least a basic understanding of how they work.

Employer Benefits

The best perk that comes with full-time employment is the chance to participate in employee benefits. Employers use these benefits to retain you, their talent, in their quest to remain competitive in a market space. Benefits range from health insurance, retirement plans, long-term incentives such as options and stock awards, commuter benefits, and many others. Some may not put dollars in your pocket directly, but do not underestimate their value. Group benefits offer significant cost savings, especially with items such as health insurance.

If you do not have direct access to employee benefits under your current scheme of employment, we will discuss options for collective benefits that may be available to you by the nature of your profession or otherwise.

Understanding the value of employer benefits will also help you move beyond your base salary and bonus to more critically evaluate future job opportunities.

Estate Planning

When you transcend this earth, what do you want to happen to the people and things most important to you? Who would make a financial or medical decision for you if you can't make one for yourself? Have you ever thought about these things?

You can bet your assets we need to cover estate planning. This piece of your financial puzzle creates certainty for our time on and off this earth, especially for committed couples and those with children. Estate planning is not a warm and fuzzy topic; it can be kind of depressing to have to contemplate things we'd rather bury in the back of our minds. But I can promise you that like the other previous themes, having your estate in order will help you sleep better at night. It will ensure you never really lose control, even when you do.

CHAPTER THREE

CHOOSING, AFFORDING, AND OWNING COLLEGE (AND GRAD SCHOOL)

Congratulations, young Millennial. You sat through Saturday morning test prep courses for six months, took the exam twice, and received a score you could live with. You spent the other weekends visiting campuses, likely with your parents, roaming through student unions and buying T-shirts you will most certainly give away if things don't work out. You worked grueling late nights on your 500-word essay about that time you faced a challenge in your life, overcame it, and ended up better for the experience. And one sunny afternoon, you opened your inbox and received the news—you're in. No matter how monotonous it all seemed before, there's no better feeling in the world.

That's how Heather describes her college application process. She applied to a dozen undergraduate universities and schlepped up and down the East Coast visiting them all, writing countless stories of overcoming adversity, and taking the SATs (three times in her case). Same went for the LSATs and applying to law school.

Things work a little differently in the state of Florida, where the state lottery system underwrites large scholarships for qualifying residents to enroll in its public universities. This means many Floridians like me stay put because the deal is just too good to pass up. I applied early admission to one school, the University of Florida, because my brother was already there and because it is the best school in the state, according to me and everyone else who ever went there. As someone who now preaches investment diversification, I will admit that my strategy was anything but diversified. What if I didn't get into my one and only choice? I guess I would have had to apply to that *other* Florida state school in Tallahassee, heaven forbid.

I recognize these were craft beer problems in a world of Bud Light—I was very lucky. If I had to select my school like a "choose your own adventure" book, the way so many people do, I would not have had a single clue which direction to go. Like many impressionable young people, I probably would have been persuaded by the flash and awe, and believed that attending any college that made me feel good was my right instead of a privilege. It's very difficult to possess the maturity, let alone the foresight to make such a huge decision alone. Without a no-brainer option like Florida, I admittedly would have fallen into the same problem other Millennials did. I just wasn't equipped to act otherwise.

People say that getting admitted is the hardest part. I beg to differ.

Now that you've been admitted, this chapter will teach you about *your* selection process. The methods by which you select and afford college or graduate school could prevent you from making the first—and potentially the largest—financial misstep of your life.

The place to start your selection process is by understanding the potential cost as best you can. It's time to put your thinking caps on because class is about to begin.

THE COST OF EDUCATION IS TOO DAMN HIGH!

People need a college degree to compete in today's marketplace. Aside from a couple of Zuckerberg-level tech savants, people hoping to compete and live prosperously today are attending college. Sure, "prosperity" is relative, but without a doubt, one thing is true: college degrees command greater earning power.

According to a 2014 report, Millennial college graduates ages 25 to 32 earn an average estimated $17,500 more per year than individuals with just a high school diploma.[1] In today's dollars, that amounts to an additional $525,000 through a 30-year career.

Graduate degrees widen the income gap even further. According to "The Economic Value of College Majors," a 2015 study by Georgetown University, individuals with a graduate degree earn on average $17,000 more annually during the course of a career than those with just a bachelor's degree. In today's dollars, that amounts to another $510,000 through a 30-year career.[2]

On its face, the equation seems simple: invest in your education and make more money. Assume the risk and obtain the reward.

But educating yourself costs a lot of money. Not *popping bottles on the weekend* money or even *Louis Vuitton luggage* money. I am talking *down payment on a house* money. For four-year programs, the average published undergraduate charges for the 2016–2017 school year were $33,480 at private nonprofit colleges, $9,650 for in-state residents at public colleges, and $24,930 for out-of-state residents at public colleges.[3] The average annual cost of tuition for a graduate degree totals nearly $11,000 at public schools and $23,000 at private schools.[4]

Using some loose math, the average price of a four-year college program can cost nearly $90,750, and a two-to-three-year graduate program can cost between $22,000 and $69,000. This doesn't even include living expenses, which warrant a whole separate discussion. Now that's some fancy learning!

The issue is not only the price tag itself, but also the rate in which it's skyrocketing. College tuition and fees have gone up by approximately 500 percent since 1985.[5]

Here's some perspective on how insane that is. The Consumer Price Index ("CPI"), which measures the change in price of consumer goods and services, rose 115 percent during the same period. Meaning, the cost of education increased almost *five times* more than the cost of everyday things you buy. Taken at its simplest level, students are paying much more to receive the same (if not less) value for their college education than their car, groceries, and haircuts—all which cost more with time, but have not inflated nearly to this extent.

But *why* has the cost of education ballooned?

The answer depends on who you ask.

Institutions say that a widespread decrease in public funding has forced their hand to push essential operating costs onto their students. They argue that they need to raise tuition to recruit and retain tenured professors with competitive salaries. However, full-time faculty is barely making more money than in the 70s, and that's not even considering inflation. College administrators, on the other hand, have managed to achieve seven-figure-salary status, and there are more administrative positions today than ever before. Overall, the funding itself seems to be doing all right; certainly, better than decades ago. State funding reached an inflation-adjusted high of $86.6 billion in 2009. And the federal Pell Grant program has grown to an adjusted $34.3 billion per year, up from $10.3 billion in 2000.[6]

The institutions could state more accurately that funding hasn't decreased—it just hasn't kept up with student enrollment. According to the National Center for Education Statistics, total fall enrollment numbers peaked in 2010 at a little more than 21 million.[7] That was right in the initial recovery stages of the Recession. At a core time for the Millennial demographic to be entering college or graduate programs, enrollment was at its highest. Even if public funding increased at a reasonable rate, the subsidies could not keep up with this demand to attend. Therefore, funding per student dropped as the class sizes grew.

The money would have to come from somewhere else. So, the cost of education rose for Millennials because more of them wanted—or needed—to be educated.

And we are barely shoveling into the topsoil here. We need to dig deeper.

Let's return to the idea about Millennials receiving a return on their investment. In theory, the more expensive it is, the harder it will be to receive that positive return. And we all know it's not that simple. Different colleges work for different people for different reasons. Indeed, higher education is not a "one size fits all" tank top: just because you're wearing one doesn't mean you should be.

In other words, what makes sense for some people may not make sense for others. Each institution has its pros and cons. Evaluating them is one of the hardest things for young Millennials to do, especially if they aren't enabled with financial knowledge.

Let's go over what some of those pros and cons might be.

Receiving your education at an in-state public university is cost-effective. Their tuitions are often the most affordable, and state residents might be able to benefit from exclusive financial aid and scholarship programs. In some cases, attending a public university as an out-of-state student could *still* be cheaper than going private. If the school is close to home and commuting is an option, you can save another boatload on housing costs, as well.

But public universities most clearly showcase the issue with high student enrollment and dollars invested per student. As of the fall of 2015, out of the 10 universities with the highest undergraduate enrollment numbers, nine are public. None of them ranked within the top 50 of the *U.S. News & World Report's* 2017 Best Colleges. University of Central Florida topped the list with 54,513 students.[8] That's a ton of seats in each classroom and caps to compete with at graduation. Professor-student relationships are tougher to foster if you can't get near the lecture podium. Even with large alumni networks, they are often impersonal and hard to leverage in the workforce unless you make extraordinary efforts to stay involved (I can attest to this firsthand). In other words, there is a greater probability of you being a number than a name.

Then, there are the elite private institutions: the Ivies and even the baby Ivies. Their names carry such great weight that some would argue they provide you with an "insurance policy" for your future. More intimate classroom sizes can facilitate important contact with top professors, many of whom are leaders in their fields and can offer valuable mentorship before and after graduation.

But the expense of going private can be overwhelming. Columbia University and Vassar College top the list of most expensive private colleges for the 2016–2017 school year at approximately $55,000 and $53,000 per year, respectively. Even if the names carry incredible prestige, a student without direction can easily squander that opportunity. Exploring a loose topic of interest, diving down a philosophic rabbit hole, or pondering the meaning of life won't support even the brightest student after graduation. Imagine you borrowed more than $200,000 in student loans for these majors:

- *Folklore and Mythology from Harvard University.* It turns out this program provides the talent for all the UFO shows on The History Channel.

- *Egyptology at Columbia University.* Pyramids are cool and all, but the only larger waste of money was the actual construction of the Great Pyramids!

- *Visual Studies: Art and Culture of Seeing Concentration at the University of*

Pennsylvania. Better get your eyes checked before enrolling.

You catch my drift. Attending an esteemed private university is something to be incredibly proud of, but if you're footing the bill, you better make the most of it.

Finally, there are the lowest-tiered private colleges and universities, which I deem a trap. If the diluted training from an overenrolled public university had a baby with the extravagant cost of an elite private institution, you would be left with the redheaded stepchild of college education—the schools that, no matter how you cut it, are never the most financially responsible choice (unless they're paying you to attend).

I will not name names, because I do not need to. Run your finger down the most recent *U.S. News & World Report* rankings and check out the exorbitant cost of some schools near the bottom. Those schools will not provide you the studies, resources, or recruiting clout that higher-tiered schools will, yet they charge just as much if not more. You are paying for a very expensive tank top, and years from now, that won't be such a cool story, bro.

Now, I didn't just throw shade at these colleges without good reason. I did it to illustrate how each institution has its own set of good and bad that you need to evaluate. Where the tipping point lies between the cost of a specific university's degree and the actual return on your investment is complicated because it requires you to evaluate your honest, personal goals in life, and take ownership over them at a young age. It also requires you to be responsible. Not all Millennials were ready to do that before applying to college or graduate school.

I am not writing this to be a dream crusher. I believe that it would be great for everyone to have their chance to reach their highest degree of excellence, wherever they want, and be the best [insert your career here] that they can be. But unfortunately, a world where everyone could have that chance would be a sunshine and rainbows utopia—not the real world that we live in.

In 2015, President Barack Obama unveiled a proposal to make a two-year associate's degree free and available to any American who wanted it. In announcing his plans, he said that college education should be "as free and universal as high school is today."[9] Of course, the plan would have been expensive, costing the federal government *$60 billion*, with a "b." Without knowing President Donald Trump's formal position on higher education issues, I have a feeling a proposal like this one won't make it into the Oval Office or Mar-a-Lago.

This might not top the federal agenda anymore, but now, states like New York are pursuing the idea. Governor Andrew Cuomo with U.S. Senator Bernie Sanders announced a first-of-its-kind proposal for 2017 that would make college tuition free for more than 940,000 of New York's middle-class at The State University of New York and The City University of New York. Governor Cuomo said, "[a] college degree is not a luxury—it is an absolute necessity for any chance at economic mobility . . . ."[10] The Excelsior Scholarship, as it's called, mandates that students must attend school full-time, which will support graduation rates and result in students incurring less student loan debt for living and other expenses. The City of San Francisco is planning to give tuition-free community college a shot, as well.

In a sense, governments win by holding our education out as a right. The more educated our nation becomes, the more competitive we will be with the world and with ourselves. We would stimulate our economy and everyone would win. Sunshine and rainbows, right?

Maybe in a country where there's more Bernie Sanders(s). Until state or federal subsidies exist on a broader scale, we need to stop being so naïve.

The colleges and universities have their own reasons for wanting us educated. These institutions are businesses, many of which are privately held. Like any other brand, they compete for our money, often with a focus on how wonderful it feels to be a part of it all. Showcasing Division I sports, glistening new buildings, and student life on campus, they place much emphasis on *community* and the ease to fit into it. The community—above much else—is what fuels the collegiate brand. Why else would kids pay $160,000 to attend a less-prestigious university than the better state school 20 minutes from home?

Above all else in this chapter, let this point mean something to you. Institutions cannot sell you on their brand without selling you on the most crucial point of all: *that attendance is affordable.* Whether you are the son of a real estate tycoon in Manhattan or the daughter of a Wal-Mart employee in the Rust Belt, you should feel just as able to become a part of The University family. Because the entire enterprise fails unless these institutions can make their programs feel affordable to anyone.

The longer we get sold on viewing higher education as a right—not a privilege we must figure out how to pay for—the more we will get sold on how affordable it is to pursue it. And it isn't affordable. The government's starting to say it, but most schools aren't.

The access to student loans makes it all possible: the ability to attend the college of your choice and the opportunity to be charged more to do so. *Even you can become one with The University, for four easy installments of $27,000—with financing available for all!*

There is a fundamental problem with the rising cost of education. But until the paradigm shifts, the costs are the Millennial's reality. More critical than the cost alone, however, is that most young people must decide how to fund that cost without understanding the consequences.

THE COSTS TO CONSIDER

First, we will review the set costs. The largest set cost is your tuition per semester. This base number will not vary too much during your studies if you will be taking a similar number of credits per semester. Some schools charge tuition by credits, whereas others do not. As discussed earlier, tuition varies greatly from school to school and from student to student. But as a general rule, public universities cost less, especially for state residents.

There are other sneaky sister costs to consider here, which I consider sneaky because you can't avoid paying most of them. These are the fees. Lots of them. These also vary greatly from school to school, and you may have a hard time figuring out what they all are. And don't ask me, because as far as I'm concerned, many of these fees are probably just redirected away from tuition to keep those numbers looking steady. But some examples include: student activity fees, health fees, technology fees, energy fees, "fees" fees.... The moral of the story here is that the cost of tuition alone never represents the full picture. You must also consider fees. If you are not provided with a breakdown in your admissions materials, call or write the registrar's office to obtain more information.

The second category of costs you will have while supporting yourself in school is room and board. Lodging can be really affordable or really expensive depending on a number of factors. Does the school offer on-campus housing, and how many students are accommodated there? For example, Heather's law school technically offered on-campus housing in Manhattan, but it only could accommodate a small percentage of enrolled students at the time. If on-campus housing won't be available to you, is the school within commuting distance to your home, or will you rent an apartment nearby? If you must rent an apartment, do some research on the average costs in that geographic area. There's a disparity between the costs to live near campus in, say, Madison, Wisconsin (the University of Wisconsin) and Coral Gables, Florida (the University of Miami).

Nourishment is also considered part of your room and board costs. Does the school offer a student meal plan? This is often the most affordable way to dine. Ask yourself how much you like to eat and when, because some schools offer both unlimited meal plans and debit card style options. If your school does not offer a meal plan, understand the costs of dining and groceries in the area. Obviously, there's a huge difference in food costs between small college towns and metropolitan areas. Just because you are a student in San Francisco doesn't mean you get student pricing at the corner store. And don't forget about transportation. Research whether you need to have a car to get around, or if there is reliable public or university-sponsored transportation available.

Another set of costs is books, supplies, and technology. The cost of these materials may depend less on the school and more on your coursework. For example, if you want to pursue graphic design, there might be a host of programs and applications you'll want to purchase to help you get a leg up outside the classroom. The point here is that you shouldn't dismiss these costs and must account for them in your evaluation process.

By investigating and compiling these numbers, you will take reasonable steps to understand how much your education could cost. But that's just part one.

Now, you must ask yourself the toughest question of all: *is it worth it?*

As I touched on before, calculating the return on your education investment is not straightforward like a math equation. It's a complicated interplay between knowing the financials and taking a good, solid look at yourself.

To help you figure this out, let's start by examining your career goals. Do you have them? It's okay if you don't. Lots of people don't have a clear path. But if you are struggling with what you want to pursue, that should absolutely factor into how much you spend. I'd argue you should spend less money to pursue the unknown. Expensive private educations are a luxury; this goes for undergraduate and graduate school degrees.

Take it from Heather, who spent a ton of money studying to become a lawyer when she didn't know a thing about practicing law. Her first plan was to become Ari Gold from *Entourage*, then a Big Law associate, then a state prosecutor, then just about anything with health benefits. If she wasn't certain what she wanted out of attending law school, she should have chosen a program that was more affordable because she was footing the bill. At the very least, this would have lightened the pressure after school while she figured it out (it being life).

If you do have specific career aspirations, it's great that you have a profession to conduct your research around. Let's say you want to pursue fashion merchandising. I know nothing about this field, but hey, it sounds cool. You have been accepted into two universities with comprehensive fashion merchandising programs—one at your resident state's public university and one at a private institution in New York City.

The one closer to home would afford you in-state tuition at approximately a third of the cost; however, the private city school offers what you believe to be unparalleled access to design houses and real opportunities for internships and eventual employment. It also, undeniably, has a better name and reputation. But graduates rise or fall every day from even the most elite institutions, so you need to think with the end in mind. Attending the objectively better school doesn't rubber-stamp your future for success. If you are going to pay a lot more money to attend that school, you need to become very familiar with your appetite for risk and what the real reward looks like on the other end.

Take your research to the next level. Think about the specific industry you would like to break into after your studies and look into the average starting salary for that industry, as well as where the jobs in that industry are located. Understanding these factors will go a long way when "calculating" the value that you can extract from a specific degree from a specific university.

The rising fashionista learned that she would most definitely want to move to New York City after studying fashion merchandising in college. However, the starting salary would not be very high and things would certainly be tight, given the cost of living. She decided it would be less risky to attend her in-state public university, so that she would not have to borrow as much money. Maybe she could pursue a summer internship in the city, which seems like more of an opportunity and less of a risk. She knows she would have to work a little harder to make industry contacts, but the payoff in savings would be huge and help her start her life after school. She is making an emotionally honest, well-reasoned decision. And I, as her financial advisor, agree with her.

Your career isn't the only factor to consider when asking yourself, "Is it worth it?" Even though I'm a numbers guy, there are more soft factors at play, which come second in your value analysis but should not be disregarded. These include things such as geographic location, proximity to family, demographic, social programs, and even the accessibility to Division I sports. Was it always your dream to attend, or are family or friends just pressuring you? I am not here to tell you which of these things to care about, or that you should or shouldn't care about them. Contemplate everything that is important to you—yes, even how the school just makes you *feel*—because regret is a terrible feeling to experience after shelling out thousands of dollars. That's called buyer's remorse, and it sucks.

So, congratulations again, young Millennial. You've decided to attend a college that is not Florida State University. You're already off to a great start!

But really, you are off to a great start. You understand what the cost of your education will be, and you have carefully determined that you are comfortable because you are choosing the right program for you.

Yet, a big question remains.

How Will You Pay For It?

Here is a quick overview of your potential sources of funding.

Parental or family support is money provided by the ones who love you. Don't ever take it for granted, and don't spend it all in one place!

College savings of your own. *Let the hustle flow through you.* Good for you for saving money to fund your own education. Even if it's not enough to pay for your entire tuition, it may help with your living expenses and discretionary purchases. You will read more about cash flow during college in the next chapter.

Private loans are another way to source money for your education. You borrow these loans from private banking institutions. The terms may be better than student loans offered by the federal government, but they could also be less flexible if you fall into financial hardship. It all depends on those terms. Read with caution.

Financial aid. This is money to assist you in paying for your education. There are many forms of financial aid afforded by public or private organizations, federal and state governments, and the college institutions themselves. Some must be repaid and some need not. To obtain any sort of federal student aid, you must fill out a Free Application for Federal Student Aid ("FAFSA"). Here are the options:[11]

Scholarships or grants. Free money for outsmarting people. Actually, academic achievement is only one way to obtain scholarships or grants. Showing leadership skills or performing social good may also get you recognized and land money in your pocket. There are hundreds of thousands of scholarships in this country, ranging from a couple of hundred bucks to full-tuition coverage. It's amazing how many of these scholarships go unclaimed because students do not know they exist or do not believe they are competitive for them. Give it a shot and apply. You just might surprise yourself.[12]

Work-study. There are government-run programs that provide part-time employment to students. In return, these programs fund a portion of your education.

Student loans are the gasoline fueling the fire of the Millennial Problem. The William D. Ford Federal Direct Loan Program provides various types of loans under which the federal government is your lender. The most important to know are:

1. **Direct Subsidized Loans** are available to undergraduate students who demonstrate financial need. The federal government pays the

interest on these loans during school (as long as you are enrolled at least part-time), for the first six months after graduation and during a period of deferment. Importantly, undergraduate federal student loans are capped at $57,500 per student. Only $23,000 of that capped amount may be subsidized.

2. **Direct Unsubsidized Loans** are available to undergraduate and graduate students. You don't need to demonstrate financial need to get them, and interest accrues from the onset of when you borrow them, capitalizing—or adding—on top of the amount you originally borrowed. The amount you originally borrowed is called the principal.

3. **Direct PLUS Loans** can be taken out by graduate students ("Grad PLUS Loans") or parents of dependent undergraduate students ("Parent PLUS Loans"). They have no aggregate or cumulative limit up to the school-designated "Cost of Attendance," making these especially dangerous for naïve prospective students trying to pay for expensive graduate programs.

4. **Direct Consolidation Loans** is what your loan would be called if you consolidated all your federal loans into one giant loan. When you consolidate loans of varying amounts and interest rates, you are left with one consolidated interest rate somewhere in the middle.

We will discuss whether consolidation makes sense for you in the next chapter. But know this now: amassing student loan debt from the loan options just listed can be more dangerous than other types of debt. Please let these next few paragraphs sink in.

Unlike borrowing for a tangible thing like a home, a car, or a mattress, student loans and their interest rates are valued by collateralizing your future earning potential. If you can't pay the piper, your brain can't be seized or repossessed. This big difference drives the following perilous characteristics of student loans.

First, current interest rates for federal student loans are currently between 3.76 and 5.31 percent. But for many Millennial graduates who have already borrowed for their college education, those rates can be as high as 8 percent. In many cases that's higher than current mortgage rates. For unsubsidized loans, interest accrues while the student is still learning, often underemployed, and unable to make payments during school. At graduation, the student receives a bill much higher than the cost of tuition, so high that most first payments on unsubsidized loans are interest only. The higher the interest rate, the more interest that must be paid across the life of the loan, and the longer it will curtail one's ability to move forward in life.

This next point really bugs me. Student loan payments are not tax deductible if your adjusted gross income exceeds $80,000. Even if you do qualify, the amount you can deduct is capped at $2,500. Except for the very wealthy, people who take out business loans or mortgages can typically deduct substantial loan interest on their annual tax filings. These tax deductions are significant incentives that put money back in the borrowers' pockets for ultimate savings. People seek education to earn more money. A salary of $80,000 or more may seem considerable, but not in the face of the six-figure student debt held by a doctor, lawyer, or other professional with an expensive graduate degree. When tax incentives exist for the purchase of million-dollar homes, it seems suspect that the benefit for student loan borrowers would be capped by an arbitrary salary amount, especially when many graduates who are earning that kind of salary had to amass significant debt to jumpstart their careers. How do you think Heather felt when her first job offered her $81,000, just barely more than the cap?

Federal student loans are also not dischargeable in bankruptcy, except for extreme circumstances. To get rid of them, you must either repay them or die. Although I do not view bankruptcy as a real vehicle to implement one's financial goals, it is an option of last resort, and by taking that away from the student borrower, the government takes away that last resort. Rather than allow you to file for bankruptcy on your student debt, the government will garnish your wages, seize your tax refunds, intercept government benefits, sue you to access your assets, and destroy your credit. In other terms, there is no path they will not pursue to make sure you are diligently repaying your loan, or they will hold that large debt cloud over your head until it's buried six feet underground.

But what about highly touted, super-flexible income-driven repayment plans, such as Income-Based Repayment ("IBR")? Qualification for income-driven plans is based on a calculation of your debt-to-income ratio. Once you qualify, your required monthly payment would be significantly less than that under the 10-year or 30-year standard repayment plan. Sounds cushy, right?

I wouldn't get too excited.

An extended repayment option may offer flexibility by easing your cash flow today, but you need to consider the long-term consequences. Paying just $60 per month on a $100,000 loan, when the interest on that $100,000 is accruing at 6.5 percent, sets up a situation where your monthly payment doesn't even come close to touching the principal of the loan. And any plan that lets you pay less than the monthly interest amount is working you further into debt, rather than out of it.

It is true that income-driven plans offer complete loan forgiveness to some. Specifically, graduates who pursue jobs in the public sector and make timely payments for 10 years will have their loans completely forgiven, tax-free. Otherwise, qualifying graduates who make timely payments will have their loans forgiven in 20 or 25 years, but with a ginormous tax bill at the finish line.

Here is the real kicker. Income-driven plans require annual qualification. Technically, this means that you either must: (a) stay employed in the public sector for 10 years, which is a real commitment and requires you to lock in a decade of your life at all costs; or (b) never earn too much money during the course of those 20 or 25 years, or you will no longer qualify. Should you not fully submit to the income-driven process in one of these two ways, you will eventually lose your qualification status and be stuck with thousands of more dollars in interest from paying so little for so long. Sure, income-driven plans provide helpful short-term solutions to borrowers in need. But perhaps an unintended consequence is that it disincentivizes borrowers from ever reaching too high, or they will be in even more trouble just when they thought they got out of the red. That's the opposite of the American dream.

You may have thought your admission letter sealed the deal, but it was just the first step. You should take careful consideration of the costs and returns of your prospective program before pulling the trigger. Your older self will thank you.

Cash Flow and Easy Mac

You've gotten admitted, selected your school, and figured out how to pay for it. Amazing. Once your bright eyes and bushy tail show up on campus, though, here is how you truly own it.

The most important financial theme to embrace in your collegiate years is cash management. Intimately understanding how money flows in and out of your life is the foundation for making good decisions, whether you're a student or not.

Managing your money starts with cash flow. You will work up your cash flow all the time (remember: it's *fluid*). The way to approach cash flow as a full-time student is a little different than how to approach it during your working years, but the principles remain the same. The basic cash flow equation is:

Income − Expenses = Savings (or Deficit)

Let's examine each piece.

Income is money coming in. Typically, you earn income from being employed. During college and graduate school, however, you can also fundamentally consider as "income" what you receive in the form of student loans, financial aid, scholarships, work-study programs, and support from your parents.

Expenses are money going out. You incur expenses to support yourself. They are either fixed, meaning they stay the same each month or year (such as rent or tuition), or they are variable, meaning they change each month or year (such as clothing or food).

Savings are whatever is left over when your income is greater than your expenses. Savings help to fund your financial goals and Great Things in Life.

A **deficit** occurs when your expenses are greater than your income. Cash flow deficits result in you mounting debt or losing your savings.

While in school, cash flow is very expense-focused because students usually are not working full-time jobs or focused on saving money. The main priority is to do well academically and get by while doing it. By looking at expenses first, it's easiest for a student to back into what he or she needs to earn as income to support a desirable lifestyle. Later on, I will modify this lesson for when you are earning a salary.

Start by listing all your fixed expenses, such as your room and board, tuition, fees, cell phone bill, and so on. I suggest reflecting each expense as a monthly one.

After you've listed them, determine how much money you need each month to live a lifestyle comfortable enough to focus on your education. These make up your variable expenses.

What is comfortable enough? Only you can answer that, but I urge you to be honest with yourself about what's reasonable and what's excessive. Sure, you need to clothe yourself, but a wardrobe that's diverse in price goes a long way. Ladies, for what it's worth, Heather has always been a huge believer in the notion that designer bags make cheap shirts look expensive. Try it and save yourself a boatload on tops that will only get beer spilled on them anyway. Don't forget jeans at the Gap, because they're always on sale. And sure, you need to eat, but making use of the school meal plan—no matter how gnarly the salad bar looks—is sure cheaper than spending $12 per quinoa bowl down the block. Oh, and Easy Mac. Lots of Easy Mac.

How you choose to spend money on variable expenses directly affects how to finance your education, especially when you're borrowing money to do it. That money may feel free today, but trust me, it won't tomorrow.

Examples of Fixed and Variable Expenses

Fixed

Student loan repayments

Mortgage or rent payments

Utilities (for example: water, gas, electric, cell phone, cable, and Internet)

Property taxes

Insurance premiums

Car lease payments

Variable

Food

ATM withdrawals

Transportation and fuel

Subscriptions and memberships (for example: fitness classes, magazines, and streaming services)

Personal care (for example: grooming, glasses, and contacts)

Medical costs

Child care

Clothing

Entertainment

Hobbies

Travel

Gifts/donations

Once you have all your variable expenses written down, add them up to calculate your monthly living expense. This is an important number because it dictates how much money you will need to bring in each month from your sources of income.

For example, if you figure your expenses are $2,500 per month, and you receive $500 per month from your parents and another $500 per month from financial aid and part-time work, you're going to need another $1,500 each month to support yourself. You might decide to borrow the extra money, feeling confident your grades will land you a great job in your field. Perhaps you'd rather pick up some additional work and reduce your variable expenses so you don't have to borrow at all.

On that note, if you needed to take out student loans to jumpstart your college education, you can use your cash flow analysis to figure out how much you need to borrow each semester. Maybe with proper planning, it's less than you thought.

And with that, you've introduced yourself to the basic art of cash flow. Well done, grasshopper. Now, I want to touch on an important opportunity afforded to young motivated students.

Even for those fortunate enough to study without borrowing money, you can improve your quality of life by working. Paid internships or part-time work can supplement your cost of living and give you financial flexibility to have a little more fun or save for later. Alternatively, internships for college credit can be thought of as deferred income. They are a wonderful investment in your training and experience for a future field of study.

In college, I spent a considerable amount of time outside the classroom learning about the financial services industry by working with my dad. And I have to give the guy some credit. Truth be told, I didn't just wake up one day and think it would be an awesome idea to spend 20 hours a week working in his satellite office learning the finer points of small business ownership. In fact, I distinctly remember spending at least one dehydrated Friday morning sleeping under my desk with my head in a trashcan, only to do it again later that night. Alas, I wish I appreciated the opportunity more at the time, and I thank my dad for gently nudging me through it. What I learned from him in that job provided me the necessary leverage to afford—all by myself—to move to New York City at 24 to start building a financial planning business of my own.

Had I been financially empowered from the start, I wouldn't have needed his gentle nudging. By understanding something as fundamental as cash flow, I would have known better what I'd need to live my life *after* school, which would have dictated how I spent my time and energy *during* school. Would I have studied harder and partied lighter? Debatable. But I would have had my eyes wide open while doing it.

In addition to mastering cash flow and seizing good opportunities, you should use your college years to build credit. Credit provides you access to financing for homes, cars, businesses, and more. The better your credit, the better terms you receive when borrowing money for these things. To start building your own credit, try applying for a credit card at your local bank. It might be easier to gain approval if you already have an account there. If you are unable to obtain a credit card of your own, find out if you can become an authorized user on a parent's credit card. Be sure to pay off your balance in full each month and on time. It's important that you don't open or close too many lines of credit at once, or let your first card sit idle in your sock drawer. The point is to regularly use it to demonstrate your creditworthiness.

When I was a freshman, I opened a Blue for Students American Express Card. I was offered a whopping $600 line of credit, enough to only do a little bit of damage. I used it frequently and treated it almost like a debit card, making sure that I paid my bill in full each month. At the end of each year, I would request an increase in my credit line, having demonstrated to the credit card company that I was disciplined and responsible enough to wield a higher amount. By the time I graduated, I had a $20,000 line of credit and the beginnings of a solid credit history. Boom.

As you read earlier, I did some things right and some things wrong during those crazy years. Everyone does. Injected with our first dose of liberation, we are so pliable, so impressionable, and bound to make mistakes. But if you do the homework just outlined, don't squander your open doors, and don't get arrested, you'll be able to limit those mistakes to the little ones that can be removed with a pair of scissors.

CHAPTER FOUR

PAYBACK TIME

My wife Heather is the perfect illustration of the student loan crisis.

You may want to sit down for this.

As of January 2017, Heather had $211,694.20 in student debt. That's right; Heather is the Millennial Problem and she wants you to know it. Before passing judgment (and wondering how she married a financial advisor), let's examine how she got there.

Heather and I met during freshman year at the University of Florida. Aesthetically speaking, we were opposites: I, a clean-shave-and-polo-type guy from sunny South Florida, and she, a Birkenstocks-and-tie-dye-type girl from the Philadelphia area. Heather inherited approximately $120,000 from her late grandfather to fund her college education. She knew that this generous gift could cover her entire education at a public university, or part of her education at a private college. She chose the more conservative route, hoping to have money left over at graduation to build her adult life.

Heather became a state resident of Florida and saved tons of money on tuition. She lived comfortably, but not extravagantly (her 1998 Nissan Altima, named Thomas The Engine That Can't, had a duct-taped front headlight and couldn't exceed 60 mph without shaking like a scared little boy). To complete her bachelor's degree in journalism, she didn't borrow any money and graduated debt free, with a few dollars to spare.

As the only child of divorced parents, Heather's main goal after college was to make enough money to become financially independent. She didn't want to rely on anyone and looked forward to being an "adult," for whatever that meant. This caused her great angst because she wanted to become a journalist, but was worried it wouldn't get her there fast enough. Doing what she thought was a safer bet for her future, she took the LSAT and applied to law schools around the country. Heather has always been uber-competitive, so the list included many expensive private institutions. When the thick envelopes came in, the one she fell in love with happened to be in New York City.

She was ecstatic, but terrified. She knew that the cost of tuition at this law school, as well as the living expenses, would be higher than anywhere else; it was unlike anything she had ever dealt with before. So, when they went to visit the school, Heather and my father-in-law sought additional guidance. They sat down with the school's financial aid officer to review costs and determine whether attending seemed like the right move. The aid officer was quick to reassure Heather and her dad that financing would be available for the total cost of attendance, including anticipated living expenses. She showed them how much that would be. The financial aid officer then provided them with data on the starting salaries for graduates pursuing private legal practice. The numbers were well into six figures—more money than Heather ever imagined making at her first job. A summer associate gig at a big law firm would almost certainly cover at least one year's tuition, and she would have the rest of the loans paid off in no time.

The proposition seemed very risky. But through her whole life, Heather had risen to challenges, competed, and won. Borrowing money to jumpstart a high-paying legal career seemed like nothing more than an aggressive investment. Sure, she wasn't used to playing such a wild hand, but if not then, when?

That was in 2007. Heather's law school class was scheduled to take part in on-campus recruiting with dozens of employers in August and September of 2008, right when the markets crashed. Suddenly, summer associate classes diminished in size or were cancelled altogether. Public service offices froze their budgets. The Career Services department was paralyzed. No one was getting a job.

Thankfully, Heather was very good at writing law school exams and at being interviewed. She graduated with honors, and with the little chance she had, managed to be one of a fraction of the class to graduate with full-time employment. The job paid $81,000, far less than those on the financial aid office's idealistic data sheet. Her bi-weekly salary couldn't even cover the interest that was accruing on her loans. Forget about living expenses. This was New York City, after all.

So began her saga of many years: chasing salaries to stay afloat, diminishing her true passions in life, and failing to acknowledge why she went to law school in the first place—a question she only now can answer in earnest, the way she did earlier—all while making payments of $1,775.43 per month for the next 30 years.

The whole recession thing didn't help, either.

Heather's tale is a cautionary one, but let it be known that I am not someone who thinks all loans are bad. That would be ridiculous. Utilizing credit and incurring debt greases the economic wheel. Banking systems worldwide take on debt to keep their engines running. Businesses use credit to facilitate and expand their operations while individuals, like you and me, rely on loans for financing major purchases like homes, vehicles, and of course, higher education.

Did Heather make a huge mistake? It's not as simple as saying "Hell yeah, she did." Had she understood the consequences of her actions at the outset and coupled them with the emotional honesty to answer whether the degree was truly worth that risk, she could have made a more calculated financial decision. And we both would have avoided many sad nights and hard conversations.

When it comes to debt, I often see two types of people.

I like to compare these people to two types of birds. There are the eagles, who are too proud to bear the burden of their debt, and willing to throw every available dollar at their liability, even if it means extreme sacrifice. How noble! Then there are the ostriches, those who stick their heads deep into the dirt, burying their reality in hopes that it will all just go away. For them, it never will.

This chapter will show you what I showed Heather: that you don't need to be an eagle or an ostrich. Both birds represent extremes, and extremes don't fit comfortably into anyone's life. I will provide you with a way to think about student loan repayment in a manner that coincides with your specific financial needs, so that you can increase your chances of reaching your goals without going to extremes.

Let's fly. *Caacawww!*

GETTING ORGANIZED

Before you dive into understanding your student loans, you must get organized. This way, you can view your debt situation in its entirety. I understand that some of you might be coming off a four-year bender and have misplaced those loan confirmation documents. Not to worry; they won't forget about you.

Either just after you've graduated or when you are finishing your final credit hours, you will start receiving notifications about your initial loan payments coming due. These notifications are often replete with confusing gibberish and lots of numbers.

You will want to review the outstanding balance of each loan and separate which loans are federal and which are private. Then, learn the interest rate associated with each loan, the repayment term of each loan, and the monthly payment for each loan. Creating a table like this helps:

	Loan One	**Loan Two**
Bank/ Institution	U.S. Department of Education	Big Bank of Boston
Balance	$10,549	$20,749
Federal or Private	Federal– Unsubsidized	Private

Interest Rate	4.5% Fixed	2.99% Variable
Loan Term	10 years	7 years
In Grace Period?	No	No

Federal loan borrowers might receive notification that their loans are being sent off to a different service provider. This confuses matters more. Since Heather graduated from law school, her federal student loans changed providers twice, the second time more effortlessly than the first. If you cannot locate your federal student loans or who is currently servicing them, you can view all the information relating to them in a central database, the National Student Loan Data System.[1] Create an online account and everything should be there. After creating an online account, you will be able to view all your federal student loans and the details of each of them. If you are a private borrower, you will still need to know which financial institution issued your loan. But again, chances are they won't forget about you. Ever.

You will have, at most, a six-month grace period on certain loans from the time you graduate to make your first payment, unless you seek an extension. From the moment you formally enter repayment, you are on the hook for servicing the accruing interest and eventually chipping away at the original principal.

We are going to focus primarily on repaying federal student loans. For one, this is because you have more opportunities to make strategic decisions regarding these loans. The federal student loans provide the most flexible repayment options to choose from, which include opportunities for loan forgiveness and forbearance, should you qualify or endure financial hardship. Private loans, on the other hand, are generally less flexible and are often only taken out after your options in federal loans have been exhausted.

I highly recommend that after reading this chapter, you visit the U.S. Department of Education's Website for Federal Student Aid as an additional resource. I have to admit, the federal government provides a hell of a lot more clear and useful information on this Website now than they did years ago when my and Heather's loans went into repayment. For that, the "swamp" in Washington gets a very small golf clap.

But keep that applause light. Even if the online information has gotten better, servicing your loans may prove troublesome, even frustrating at times, given the inexperienced folks hired to help you navigate this twisted world of numbers and interest rates. As just one fun example, Heather had great difficulty setting up the "auto debit" feature with one of her loan service providers, which resulted in the provider debiting her bank account several days after the due date. When she called (and waited, and waited), no one could advise her whether this late payment resulted in additional interest being passed along to her, even though the late payment was not her fault. She asked for an amortization schedule, and they not only couldn't provide one, but they didn't even know what it was. Heather and I may take perverse joy in yelling at the cable company, but this kind of incompetence is too personal and expensive to laugh about.

The point here is not to bash anyone. If anything, Heather and I have had increasingly better service during the past several years since that happened. Our takeaway is that the folks on the other end of the phone line or computer aren't financial professionals. Some of them don't fully understand the options they are reciting back to you, let alone, understand them well enough to suggest which one is best for your life. You need to take that on yourself.

Speaking of "amortization," this refers to the re-payment of a loan's principal through time. An amortization schedule illustrates, during a set period, how much of each loan payment you make goes to principal (what you originally borrowed) and how much goes to interest (what you are periodically being charged to borrow that money).

There are two main repayment lessons that you learn from the concept of amortization. First, at the beginning of repaying a loan, most of each payment consists of interest, and toward the end of repaying a loan, most of each payment consists of principal. Second, recall that even though you may have received the principal years earlier, the money is still "borrowed" until you pay it back. Therefore, the longer the term of a loan, the more interest you pay during the life on that loan. This concept is crucial to determining which repayment plan is right for you because there is a tradeoff between using longer repayment plans—therefore having lower monthly payments—and how much more money in interest you will pay during the life of the loan.

THE REPAYMENT PLANS

Before evaluating which payment plan is right for your situation, you must understand what they specifically offer, as well as their benefits and liabilities. For a complete overview of all Direct Loans and Federal Family Education Loan ("FFEL") repayment plans, visit that same Department of Education Website I mentioned earlier. But in short, here are the four main types of federal loan repayment plans you will encounter:

Standard Repayment: This is the default repayment plan for almost all federal student loans. Your monthly payments are fixed at a certain amount for up to 10 years (or up to 30 years if you consolidated your loans, as will be discussed later). Because of amortization, you will pay the least amount through time if you choose this option.

Graduated Repayment: This plan, also available for almost all federal student loans, starts payments lower than the standard repayment plan and increases usually every two years. It is designed to create less of a financial burden in your early working years and escalate as your income grows. Payments are fixed during each two-year graded period up to 10 years (and up to 30 years for consolidated loans). Again, because of that whole amortization thing, you will pay more through time than the standard repayment plan.

Extended Repayment: This plan is available for almost all federal student loans with balances of $30,000 or more. You can repay under either a fixed or graded schedule, lasting for a term of up to 25 years. Outside of income-driven repayment plans and 30-year repayment plans for consolidated loans, it provides the borrower with the most flexibility due to its smaller monthly payments. But in turn, you will pay even more with time than the standard or graduated repayment plans.

Income-Driven Repayment: If you qualify for them, these plans allow for even lower monthly payments, which are based on a percentage of your discretionary income—anywhere from 10 to 20 percent. Income-driven repayment plans can generally be used on Direct Loans, except for Parent PLUS Loans and Unsubsidized Consolidated Loans that had consolidated a Parent PLUS Loan.

Monthly payments may be lower than the other repayment plans above, so if you absolutely need to make small payments, this is your best option. But sometimes, your monthly payments under these plans are so small that they won't even cover the interest accruing on your loans each month. This is known as "negative amortization" and will cause your loans to grow, having you pay even more interest with time. Therefore, it's important to only use these plans after careful planning; otherwise, they will do more harm than good for you.

CONSOLIDATION

Consolidating your debt has its benefits. For one, it can make the debt easier to manage. The federal government makes consolidating fairly easy for its student loan borrowers through its Federal Consolidation Loans.[2]

If you borrowed money each semester, you will see that a new loan was created each and every time. So, if you borrowed money to pay for four years of undergraduate coursework in traditional semesters, you could have eight separate loans to manage, and that's assuming you borrowed only Subsidized Direct Loans. If you also borrowed Unsubsidized Direct Loans on top of those Subsidized Loans, you could have as many as 16 separate loans.

A Federal Consolidation Loan would aggregate your loans by each type of loan (Subsidized versus Unsubsidized, including PLUS Loans) into larger ones with an interest rate equal to the weighted average of all the loans in that category. They do not lower your interest rates; they simply blend the rates of all your federal loans together into their weighted average.

For cxample, if you had an outstanding Subsidized Loan of $10,000 at a rate of 5 percent and another for $10,000 at a rate of 7 percent, you would end up with one $20,000 Subsidized Consolidated Loan at 6 percent.

Lastly, Federal Consolidation Loans allow borrowers of FFEL loans (that's you, older Millennials) to utilize those income-driven repayment plans that would otherwise not be available. Basically, if you want to take advantage of the federal government's assistance, you need to do it on their terms.

One reason to refrain from federal consolidation would be that if you have loans with varying interest rates, you would lose the ability to pay off the loans with the highest rates first. For example, if you keep your loans separate, you could pay the $10,000 Subsidized Loan with the 7 percent interest rate first, thereby saving money, because that loan charges more than the other. Note that this strategy assumes you are at least making payments that cover the interest on all of them.

In addition to Federal Consolidation Loans, there are also private consolidation loans available through financial institutions such as banks and the increasingly popular financial technology companies. All consolidation is technically a form of refinancing. But private consolidation loans can offer the chance to actually *lower* the interest rate of your loan(s) based on your creditworthiness and financial fitness.

Depending on the rate assigned and term chosen, consolidating your loans privately could result in substantial savings in interest, lower monthly payments, or both. However, you will probably lose the flexibility that federal loans afford; namely, the income-driven plans and the ability to change from one repayment plan to another at any time. Before consolidating with a private lender, you must assess how comfortable you are with losing this flexibility and locking yourself into the set terms of a private loan.

But with confidence in your ability to meet your monthly obligation, private consolidation loans can dramatically improve your student debt situation. I took the plunge and refinanced my student debt with a bank's private consolidation loan, bringing my interest rate from 6.67 percent on a standard 30-year repayment plan, to 3.5 percent on a new 15-year consolidated loan. For a few dollars more each month, I sliced the term in half, saving more than $120,000 in interest during the life of my loan. For reasons including my good credit and earning potential, a bank was willing to bet on me. All in all, it was a match made in repayment heaven.

LOAN FORGIVENESS: WHAT ARE THE CHANCES?

I want to address the mysterious concept of student loan forgiveness. You can achieve this Holy Grail of Loan Disappearance by committing to an income-driven repayment plan for many years, or to a career in public service for less (but still many) years.

With income-driven repayment plans, you must re-qualify each and every year. To do this, you must furnish your federal loan service provider with proof of income, typically in the form of your most recent tax return.

You ostriches out there: *these programs are not an opportunity for you to pay as little as possible,* continuing to bury your head in the sand, hoping your loans will go away in 20 to 25 years. You are only doing yourself a lifetime of disservice by limiting yourself this way. What if, a decade from now, you are offered your dream job, and it pays so much that you no longer qualify for the plan? Your interest has ballooned on top of the principal from you coasting on your low payments for so long. See, these plans are specifically designed to provide you with maximum flexibility so that you can focus and work harder on increasing your income, afford a different repayment plan, and eventually pay your loans in full. They're not an opportunity to game the system.

You will also have a giant tax bill waiting for you at the end of the road. The amount of debt discharged is taxable as income during the year that it's forgiven. This could literally leave you with a six-figure tax bill. I'm guessing that from all the years you've suppressed your earning potential to game an income-based repayment plan, you don't have that kind of cash lying around. Now you're in it with the IRS for six-figures plus. This is the *last* place you want to be. Trust me. I'd rather owe money to a loan shark than those guys.

For those who've chosen to pursue public service, there's student-loan forgiveness for you, too. After 10 years of service in a public role (it doesn't have to be consecutive), your student loan debt is forgiven without a tax bill waiting for you on the forgiven balance. This type of forgiveness incentivizes you and honors the fact that you are a public servant, committed to doing good for your government or community. Now, I admire anyone who chooses to dedicate a decade of his or her career to the greater good. But be emotionally honest about your goals, and keep in mind that if you are neck-deep into this commitment, you might need to turn down a potentially attractive private gig.

I also want you to recognize that all these forgiveness programs are here today, but no one can promise they are here to stay. In fact, under the current administration, it's looking more each day like they won't be. A little bit of skepticism would do every Millennial some good, given what we've seen.

WHAT DO I DO?

Well, it depends on your individual situation. Just because you *can* pay a standard 10-year repayment plan doesn't mean you should. And just because you *can* extend your payments out longer or qualify for an income-driven plan, doesn't mean you should do that, either.

What you should do is revisit your goal priorities. Longer-term repayment plans can provide you with the flexibility you may need at this moment to support yourself or put more money toward other goals. But these plans must be used with caution because you will be paying more interest through the life of the loan. Nothing is free and you will pay to tap into this type of flexibility. Only you can determine if that's okay.

Upon graduating law school, Heather had no choice but to participate in an income-based repayment plan while working her first job. She could not have afforded the standard monthly repayment otherwise. When she stepped up to a higher-paying job, she continued with the income-based plan for a bit, but voluntarily made payments above her monthly amount when she could, covering the interest and a tiny bit of principal. At a time of great uncertainty with her career, she felt more comfortable keeping that flexibility as an option. It was a crutch in case things didn't pan out as planned.

Now, Heather and I pay more than our interest and into the principal of all our student loans each month. Could we be eagles and pay much more? Sure. But to do that, we would have needed to sacrifice our home savings and our current lifestyle. We are being honest with ourselves. We'd rather own a home for our baby Hazel to grow up in and attack the remainder of our student debt later. That's our choice to make, just like you get to choose what's best for you. We fully understand the cost of this choice, and so must you if you plan on becoming financially independent.

Let me keep it real for a moment, though. Heather and I aren't happy about carrying our fat load of debt around. We fantasize about having a windfall just large enough to pay it off; about how much farther our income would take us if it just all went away. But we're not ostriches. Our decision on how to address this debt was a tough one to make, and our continued effort to pay it back is a constant fire under our asses. We will always feel a sense of urgency until the day it's gone, even if we have found a way to live comfortably while it's here.

Some call it guilt; some call it motivation. Just keep in mind that you are not necessarily seeking to owe nothing as much as you are seeking control over your cash flow in a manner that makes sense for you.

CHAPTER FIVE

W-2s, W-WHAT?

School's out and it's not just for summer. No more playing dress-up on a Tuesday night or having bourbon for breakfast. No more classroom talks that inspire heated discourse, but have no true consequences. No more meal plans. No more class plans. No more plans, unless you make them for yourself. Some would say that it's time to "adult."

Not me. I find the term "adulting" pretty ridiculous. People love to slap it on tasks that any 20- or 30-something-year-old should be able to handle. You made an omelet for breakfast? *Adulting.* You paid a parking ticket? On time? *Adulting.* You went to a BYOB paint night instead of your regular jaunt? *Hashtag adulting.*

Yes, you can do these things when you're an adult. You can also probably do them when you aren't, because they aren't the things that make you one.

Because you took the time to become honest with yourself, selected the right college based on your funding and goals, became an early master of cash flow, and selected the right repayment plan for your student loans, you already started becoming an adult long ago. And if you didn't, this is the perfect time to adopt the disciplined mindset and techniques of the past several chapters and have a fresh start as you begin your career.

The working world can be exciting, but nerveracking; this is especially so for Millennials, who are faced with the challenges of an unchartered labor environment. Because things only get more complicated as you move forward in your career and life, having a solid foundation from this point on will pay off in a big way.

We are going to revisit cash management, talk taxes, study employee benefits, and introduce the concept of investments by learning when it's appropriate to make them. To tailor this toward our reality, I will cover these topics for both corporate employees and self-employed entrepreneurs like me.

CASH FLOW REVISITED

Starting your career is a huge accomplishment. It might be the first time the money in your pocket doesn't come from your parents, scholarships, or student loans. Your main source of income now derives from a salary paid by your corporate employer or from the revenue you generate from your business's goods or services. It may feel different than before, and it should—you're earning every dollar. What this money means to your life requires you to look at the concept of cash flow again.

The mechanics of cash flow that you started mastering in college are pretty much the same now. The main difference is that you aren't *backing in* to your expenses to figure out how much you need to live. You are going to use your earned income to *back out* to what you have available to either spend or save each month.

Simply put, if you're earning a salary of $45,000 per year, you have that money to make it all work. If you spend more than what you're making, you will end up either taking on debt or needing to make sacrifices. I think we can all agree that taking on debt, outside of buying a home or starting a business, is not how we achieve GTL (Great Things in Life). No sir, I don't like it.

Remember the cash flow formula?

Income − Expenses = Savings (or Deficit)

That remains the same, but a few key details have changed. See the following table:

	Income
−	Taxes
−	Fixed Expenses
−	Variable Expenses
=	Savings or Deficit

Break expenses into three categories: taxes, fixed expenses, and variable expenses. We discussed fixed and variable expenses back in Chapter 3 and listed examples, but now we've added taxes as a separate expense item because of how significant a role they now play in cash flow. For those who worked during their college years, you might already be familiar with how taxes affect your spending power (more on this in a minute).

Are the numbers tighter than you'd like? You may not earn enough income to cover the lifestyle you used to enjoy living on someone else's dime. But being uncomfortable is normal. Not all jobs or opportunities are going to provide what you need to live the same way you're used to. However, this doesn't necessarily mean you can't accept the job. If you really want the job more than you like your lifestyle, you can probably find a way to make it work. Whether that's living at home, sharing an apartment with three roommates, or convincing your family to invest in your pursuit of professional growth is for you to figure out. Sacrifice is a huge part of adjusting to the working world. This will be just the first of many times.

One way to see if your budget works is by tracking the month-end balance of your checking account. If you're on budget, you should have roughly the same amount of cash in there each month. But try to see where you end up after three or four months. Things come up, and checking your budget after only one month often doesn't say it all about your spending habits.

TAXES

Taxes are people's most hated expense. They can have a dramatic impact on how much money you take home with each paycheck. When they aren't properly planned for, they can cause serious cash flow issues, to say the least. Therefore, it's essential for you to have a basic understanding of how they work.

Money set aside for future tax collections is called *withholding*. You'll be doing it your entire working life.

For those working as an employee (also known as a "statutory employee"), you are going to complete a tax form called a *W-4* upon being hired. The W-4 is a worksheet designed to help you decide how much money should be taken from your paycheck for federal taxes. In general, this worksheet does a decent job of guiding you to a result that will have you withholding enough money from each paycheck so that you don't owe the government an exorbitant amount of money when taxes are due. And FYI, they're due on April 15th, so you might as well set an annual reminder on your smartphone now.

Depending on where you live, you might need to withhold for state and local income taxes, too. Each state will have its own version of a W-4 to help you determine the proper amount. In addition to federal, state, and local taxes being withheld, you will also pay into two federal entitlement programs that you may have heard of: Social Security and Medicare (FICA).

For you freelancers and entrepreneurs, withholding for taxes works differently because you're technically not on payroll. You are your own employer, an independent contractor if you will, and for you, withholding for taxes is on your shoulders.

Overseeing your tax withholding can be considered more flexible for both cash flow and tax planning because you can deduct various business-related expenses. But on the other hand, it can be dangerous for those who don't know what they are doing. Also, self-employed individuals may be responsible for additional taxes just for being self-employed (called a "self-employment tax"—very original). These taxes can be found at the federal, state, and local levels and they need to be accounted for just the same.

There are so many factors that play into calculating taxes. Especially for the self-employed, I am a huge advocate of hiring a trusted tax professional, preferably a certified public accountant (CPA), who can help you understand your own unique tax situation and guide you on how to best withhold throughout the year. However, if you would rather do it on your own, you can use any number of tax calculators. I like the Salary Calculator on PaycheckCity.com for calculating your tax withholding and TurboTax for filing your taxes. Once you have calculated your estimated tax expense, you can plug that into the cash flow formula.

Before we leave taxes behind, let's touch on what happens when you withhold too much or too little. A tax refund is the result of withholding too much money for taxes. On its face, the idea of getting money back from the government sounds great, but in all actuality it's not good at all. You are getting *your own* money back, just at a later point in time. Technically, you loaned the government money you could have used or saved throughout the year at a rate of zero percent. How generous of you!

Think about it this way: you don't see the federal government giving you a zero percent interest loan for your education, do you? Nope. It's not found money; it's *your* money.

The flip side of paying taxes is owing them. As you may have guessed, this is the result of not having withheld enough for taxes throughout the year. Being surprised that you owe the government a chunk of money is far from good. There is an exception, though. If you did a stellar job with tax planning (or hired a CPA that's worth their weight in abacuses), you could have anticipated that there would be a tax payment waiting for you, allowing you to put that money aside throughout the year. Preparedness is key. Improper tax planning, however, could hit your savings hard or get you in trouble with the IRS. Both are disruptive to achieving your financial goals and are a total buzzkill on your life.

Since when is zero a perfect score? With taxes, that's when. Neither owing too much money nor getting too much of your own money back is ideal. The goal is to understand what you're paying Uncle Sam, while receiving nothing back (or paying little to nothing) each year.

EMPLOYEE BENEFITS

Benefits are perks that often come with working as a corporate employee. Employee benefits range far and wide, but their chief purpose is to retain you as talent, which allows your employer to remain competitive in your industry.

The most common benefits—or "core benefits" as I like to call them—include access to health, life, and disability insurance, as well as a retirement plan, such as a 401(k) or 403(b). Paid time off, transit stipends, flexible savings accounts, dental and vision insurance, maternity/paternity leave, free or reduced-cost dining, and child care facilities are some examples of additional employee benefits, but some of these are not the norm. Hey, not everyone can work at the Googleplex and get free gourmet meals!

Here, we will focus on core benefits alone.

Health Insurance

The most coveted employer benefit is access to health insurance. At its most basic level, health insurance provides you with access to doctors, treatment, and prescriptions at a lower cost. Being insured is all but necessary, because the cost of a major medical procedure without coverage could be financially devastating. We're talking a difference in the tens of thousands of dollars for even a one-night stay at the hospital. Although universal medical insurance coverage is at the forefront of American politics and currently available for purchase via the public option, it is expensive no matter how you slice it.[1] Therefore, when your employer is offering to subsidize all or part of the premium for a decent health insurance plan, it's a big incentive.

Your employer might have several plans to choose from, all with different prices, features, and limits. This book can't account for the design and cost of all plans out there, but by breaking down the main components, you will be able to make an informed decision about which plan is right for you.

And now, a thrilling course in healthcare terminology.[2]

Premiums: These are the payments you make each month, or with each paycheck, to be a part of the plan. Your employer will provide you with the per-month or per-pay-period cost for any plan offered and tell you how much they will pick up. Most employers will deduct health insurance premiums from your paycheck on a pre-tax basis, meaning you won't pay tax on the portion of your income that was used to pay for the premium. Consider this another bonus for you.

Deductible: Some plans also require you to front a certain amount of money for medical services before your insurer pays anything. Deductibles are based on a certain time period—usually one year. For example, if your plan has a $5,000 deductible, you will need to first pay $5,000 in qualifying healthcare costs before your plan will pay for anything.

Coinsurance: This is a percentage of what you must pay for healthcare costs after you meet your deductible. Consider yourself the "coinsurer" of all your healthcare risks. Plans with coinsurance typically cover 80–90 percent of eligible costs after the deductible has been satisfied. For example, let's assume you already satisfied the $5,000 deductible. If your plan has 20 percent in coinsurance, and you incurred another $1,000 in medical expenses, you would be responsible for paying $200.

Copayment (Copay): This is an upfront payment made when you receive healthcare-related services. For example, if you are visiting a specialist, like a dermatologist, you might have to pay a flat amount, say $50, in connection with that appointment. This isn't the same as coinsurance. Often, plans feature one or the other.

In and Out of Network: Your plan could be defined or limited by doctors and facilities that are associated with your plan's network. Generally, you will receive less generous coverage for having services outside of your network. There could be a separate deductible for these services, or simply no coverage at all. It's a good idea to see what healthcare providers are in-network before selecting a plan. I'm a fan of plans that offer *some* sort of out-of-network coverage, even if it's minimal. So, if you have a skiing accident on vacation and are taken to a remote hospital, the bill might not be pretty, but with out-of-network coverage, at least it won't be devastating.

Out-of-Pocket Maximum: You're probably not having a good year if you've reached your out-of-pocket maximum. This is the most money you can possibly spend before your insurance picks up 100 percent of covered costs. Generally, this does not include premiums, but it does include just about everything else. For example, it's January 2nd, and you broke your arm breakdancing on New Year's Eve.[3] The medical bills for putting your limb back together totaled $20,000, and they were all in-network. If your deductible is $5,000, your coinsurance is 20 percent, and your out-of-pocket maximum is $7,500, the most you are going to pay is $7,500. Any covered in-network medical expenses for the rest of the year will be 100 percent covered by your plan. That's called a silver lining.

There are dozens of other terms related to health insurance, but knowing the ones just discussed will help you understand the gibberish of choosing a medical plan. Ultimately, you'll need to evaluate your overall healthcare needs alongside your cash flow to choose a plan. For those who are in tip-top shape and rarely see doctors beyond an annual physical, maybe a high-deductible plan with low premiums would be a risk worth taking for you. Indeed, it costs less if nothing happens. However, if you're prone to getting sick, have chronic illnesses, are super clumsy, or just love searching WebMD and seeing specialists, perhaps there's more economic value to choosing a plan with higher premiums and a lower deductible and coinsurance. Your goal is to find the option that best fits your healthcare needs while also keeping costs in mind.

Now, for the self-employed peeps, things are a little more complicated with your health insurance coverage. Your primary options are buying private coverage, purchasing a plan through the public option if one is available to you, joining your spouse or domestic partner's plan, or if possible, remaining on your parent's health insurance, which is currently permitted through age 26.

Unfortunately, in many instances, coverage for the self-employed (or unemployed) is more expensive and less comprehensive for the same money as those receiving health insurance through their employer. However, I suggest you look into joining professional associations within your field, many of which offer their members pooled access to benefits such as health insurance. The membership dues might be worth it.

Lastly, some coverage—no matter how poor— is always better than none. No one is invincible and accidents happen. Remember that, next time you bust a move on New Year's Eve.

Disability Insurance

At this stage in your life, one of your most important assets is your ability to earn income. Without this ability, it's impossible to achieve GTL. Therefore, a quintessential core benefit is group disability insurance.

Should you be unable to perform the duties of your job due to—you guessed it—disability, this type of insurance coverage provides a percentage of your income as a monthly benefit. Disability insurance comes in two varieties: short-term and long-term, each covering a certain period. Typically, *short-term disability* will provide you with 100 percent of your monthly wages for between two weeks and one year, depending on the plan. After that, *long-term disability* will generally cover amounts as high as 60 percent of your wages through age 65. For this section, we're going to focus on long-term disability insurance.

I highly support enrolling in any employer-provided group disability insurance. It's generally much cheaper than purchasing an individual policy on the open market. If these benefits are available through your workplace, learn more about their cost and then strongly consider enrolling as soon as possible. It's often too good of a protection planning opportunity to pass up.

Please note one detail. Pay close attention to whether your premiums for group coverage are coming out of each paycheck on an after-tax basis. (They generally are, but I've seen some cases where they are being paid pre-tax.) You will want to pay for any group disability coverage with after-tax payroll deductions, because if you ever need to collect, you would then receive that benefit tax-free. There's a big difference between 60 percent of your income and 60 percent of your income after taxes. Check your pay stub and if it isn't clear, reach out to human resources for clarification.

Once again, self-employed hustlers must fend for themselves with disability insurance coverage. As I mentioned before, disability insurance isn't cheap for individuals. The premiums for this kind of coverage are determined by an evaluation of your health and income through a process called *underwriting*. The insurance carrier collects personal and financial information through your application, medical records, blood and urine samples, and other physical measurements to determine your eligibility for coverage. It's a complicated web, so I recommend that you consult a trusted financial or insurance professional to provide you with quotes and guidance for coverage options and their associated features.

There are policies of all shapes and sizes, so it is important to understand what's out there. Should you head down the path of applying for individual coverage, know there are two general categories of disability insurance policies. They are *any occupation* (called "any-occ") and *own occupation* ("own-occ"). Any-occ policies will not pay a benefit if you become disabled and can perform *any other job* that is not your own. So, if you can flip a burger but not write computer code (your real talent), then no benefit for you. *Ouch!* Own-occ policies, however, will pay a disability benefit if you cannot perform your specific job function. Although these policies are more expensive, I find them to be worth the extra premium bucks if you can afford it. Individual policies are also portable; meaning, if you leave your job, the coverage will come with you if you continue to pay your premiums.

Again, professional associations can be a valuable resource for those not offered disability insurance through their employer or those who cannot afford or qualify for an individual policy. Also, some states like New York, New Jersey, and California have mandatory disability programs that residents pay into. Although these plans can be helpful if you become disabled, they are usually insufficient to cover most your expenses. Then again, something is better than nothing, so it's worth learning more about your state's coverage.

Disability insurance, like all insurance, is a way to reduce the fallout after something bad happens. This discussion is not meant to scare you (many advisors and agents will try to), but rather allow you to think about the risks we face every day and how to lessen them in a cost-effective way. We are all entitled to our own opinions regarding the likelihood of becoming sick or disabled.

Life Insurance

The last of our core insurance benefits is life insurance. *Life insurance* provides a death benefit to a person(s) or entity of your choice, called a *beneficiary*. Life insurance is primarily designed to replace some or all the income or "value" associated with the loss of life. Death benefits range from the hundreds of thousands to millions of dollars. Many employers provide a free basic benefit of $50,000, with the ability to purchase more in multiples of your salary. But let's stop here, because we will discuss this more later.

Retirement Plans

The purpose of any retirement plan is to allow you to invest a portion of your income now, so that you can access it in later years. There are certain tax benefits associated with the money you contribute, as well as potential chances to receive free money in the form of employer contributions. I will outline the main types of employer-sponsored plans available, how they work, the various incentives that come with them, and what's available for people without access to them.

There are three main types of employer-provided retirement plans. You may have heard of a *401(k)*, which is a tax-qualified, defined contribution retirement plan provided by a for-profit employer. *What did he just say?* "Tax qualified" means that there are tax benefits associated with participating in the plan, whereas "defined contribution" refers to the fact that you, the plan participant, defines how much goes into the plan, up to certain limits. In 2017, the most an employee under 50 can contribute to any one of these plans is $18,000 per year.

There's also a version of this plan for employees of nonprofits called a *403(b)* and one for governmental employees called a *457* plan.[4]

There are a few features that make these plans so attractive. For one, they have high contribution limits; meaning, you can put a lot of money into them each year. They are also "tax advantaged"; meaning, the money you put in can be contributed on either a pre-tax basis or after-tax basis, and it can grow tax-deferred.

For example, if you contribute 10 percent of a $100,000 salary ($10,000), you would be able to exclude that $10,000 from your taxable income. Moreover, the money in your retirement plan grows tax-deferred. Any income generated—such as the payment of dividends and interest or realized gains from the sale of investments—will not be taxed if that money remains in the plan. According to IRS rules, when you reach age 59.5, you can access this money without penalty, but when you do, distributions from the plan will be treated as taxable income. Not having to pay taxes on the plan's growth and income until distribution allows it to grow much more quickly than a nonretirement investment account when invested through a long period. This is why these types of retirement plans are *so hot right now* and always.

If you are eligible to participate, you will need to complete some enrollment paperwork or enroll online. During the enrollment process, you will be able to select the percentage of your income you wish to contribute to the plan and choose from the investment choices available in the plan. However, before contributing anything, make sure that you can afford to put money into your plan within the context of your broader goals. Sure, saving for financial independence can be a great idea, but is it a priority? Only you can answer that.

After-tax contributions, otherwise known as *Roth contributions*, work a little differently. Unlike their before-tax counterpart, these contributions are taxed as income in the year that they are made; however, they also grow tax-deferred. The big difference is that upon distribution after age 59.5, the money comes out tax-free.

So, which type of contribution is better to make? Well, that's tough to say, but it comes down to where you think tax rates will be in the future, and whether you think you'll be generating more taxable income now or in the future.

Because this is where your mind is at, right? You just wrapped your head around accepting your first job, and now you've got to become a fortuneteller, too?

As it's almost impossible to predict what tax rates will look like or what your income will be decades down the road, it might be a good idea to have a combination of both contributions, if possible. Then, you don't have to look too hard into the crystal ball.

A very desirable feature of employer-given retirement plans is the ability to receive additional contributions at the employer's discretion. We call this FREE MONEY! *Cue the marching band!* You can receive these contributions as a match to what you put in, up to a certain limit. Or you might receive an automatic contribution, generally 3 or 4 percent, just for participating in the plan.

If you are eligible to receive an employer contribution, you should jump on that free money, even if it means contributing a small portion of your salary. For example, a typical matching contribution could be something like "100 percent of your first 3 percent contributed." So, if you contribute at least 3 percent to your plan, you're going to receive another 3 percent contribution from your employer. It is important to note that some employer contributions can have a vesting schedule (or waiting period) associated with them. This protects an employer from your decision to scoot after you've gotten your free dough. Vesting schedules come in a few varieties and can last as long as five years, so be sure to see if one applies to your benefit.

For those without access to an employer-sponsored retirement plan, there are retirement savings options for you, too. If you are a statutory employee without access to a work-sponsored plan, you can contribute to a *Traditional IRA* or a *Roth IRA*, up to certain income limitations (for Roth). In 2017, individuals under 50 can contribute up to $5,500 to a Traditional or Roth Individual Retirement Account

(IRA). It's not that much compared to employer-provided retirement plans, but something is better than nothing. You already know the difference between contributing pre-tax and after-tax dollars, so those same rules apply as discussed earlier.

Things always get more complex with my self-employed hustlers. For you, there are several options available, from IRAs, to setting up your own retirement plan such as a 401(k). However, one specific retirement plan worth mentioning is a Simplified Employee Pension Individual Retirement Account, known as a *SEP IRA*.

The SEP IRA is one of the most cost-effective ways for a self-employed person with no employees to save for retirement beyond the limits of a Traditional IRA or Roth IRA. In 2017, you can contribute to a SEP IRA slightly less than 20 percent of your net profit (gross income less qualified business expenses) up to $54,000. So, for self-employed individuals with large net incomes, this would be an excellent way to save for retirement. Contributions to SEP IRAs are always pre-tax. There is no Roth option available.

Opening a retirement account of any kind or establishing your own retirement plan can be done with the help of a financial advisor, or on your own through any number of financial companies specializing in this space. It may not be too difficult, but it is time-consuming.

INVESTMENTS? NOT SO FAST (THE CASH RESERVE)

When I tell some people that I'm a financial advisor, they like to ask, "So what's a good investment these days?"

A little piece of me dies inside every time.

Although innocent, this question flies in the face of almost everything we've discussed so far. Why is this person investing money? What is he investing for? Does he think I pick stocks for a living? What is this, *Boiler Room*? I wonder if he has even earned the right to invest.

Wait. What was that?

You need to *earn* the right to invest. That's right. There are benchmarks you must hit before even discussing investments. First, you master your cash flow. If you discover you are saving money each month, that's great. Still, before you can earn the right to invest, you must almost always establish a cash reserve. Here's why.

I define a *cash reserve* as having three-to-six months of your living expenses (fixed plus variable expenses) in cash. By now, you should have an idea of those living expenses, so these numbers should not be hard to figure out. We build cash reserves so that we can protect ourselves from emergencies without having to take on debt or invade savings earmarked for other goals. We also build cash reserves to take advantage of unforeseen opportunities. The cash reserve is your cushion if things come up, because they do.

Should you allocate all your available savings toward a cash reserve before doing *anything*? Not necessarily. The right answer is a bit subjective, which is why we spent time on goal priority and need to revisit it here once again.

Let's assume that your budget reveals you can save $100/month, and this is after you can make at least the interest payments on your student loans. Besides taking advantage of matching retirement plan contributions (get the free money no matter what!), you're going to have to decide where that next dollar goes. Because we technically added a new goal to the mix—the cash reserve—you need to ask yourself, how much of a safety net do you want to have?

Again, it's goal priority, baby. You can make changes along the way when you start getting a feel for things. As you settle into your career or business, you might feel more confident and think that carrying a smaller cash reserve is okay. Or perhaps if you are nervous about job security, you will want to have more cash on hand. It's a constant evaluation that's always changing.

We covered a lot of information here, but most of it assumed that you had a job. I don't want an overarching piece of advice to get lost in the details: don't give up. If today's unchartered labor environment is preventing you from accessing your most desired career off the bat, it's okay. A diploma is no longer a meal ticket. You must rely on your creativity, agility, and flexibility to craft your own success like never before.

Just keep pushing, and do whatever you must do to stay empowered. You only slip deeper into the problem when you start feeling helpless and sorry for yourself. There's no shame in shacking up with your parents in your bright blue childhood bedroom (ahem), as long as you stay focused on your pursuit.

Nothing worth doing is easy.

Do you feel it yet? At this point, the concepts you are learning are building upon one another more and more: identifying your goals; exploring self-honesty; financing your education; managing your cash; and making smart decisions about the income and benefits that come along with employment.

I'm starting to feel good about this. Are you?

CHAPTER SIX

WEALTH IS EARNED, NOT ACQUIRED

"So, uh, Douglas, how's that nine to five treating you?"

"Nine to five," you say? That concept is funny for the young people I know in today's workforce. Those of us pursuing corporate jobs work longer hours than that, and the true entrepreneurs in our group never really have an off switch. For better or worse, technology has made it so we never need to—or hardly ever can—disconnect. We are master multitaskers, always available for our friends, family, and jobs, often all at the same time.

Distractions are only such if they affect our productivity toward something else. And if we can do both at once, is it so bad?

Like generations before us, Millennials have an entrepreneurial spirit. What separates us is our ability to harness technology to be more productive; to achieve more in the same time given.

Some Millennials discovered their entrepreneurial identity when their advanced degrees didn't align with the demands of the job market. Unemployed or underemployed, they didn't have a choice but to set out on their own. Others found traditional corporate roles to be bureaucratic, archaic, and infuriating. Even more felt like they were doing just fine, but weren't happy.

If Millennials in the workforce are guilty of one thing, it's dreaming. It's believing that we can create or offer something that could impact someone else. We don't feel *entitled* to do something important. We just understand how much smaller technology has made our world. Making an impact is more possible than ever.

All this doesn't mean you should be your own boss. Not yet, at least.

There are serious tradeoffs in becoming an entrepreneur. Although you hope to achieve limitless success, you are making a huge gamble. Foregoing your salary welcomes the peril of instability at any time—at *terrible* times. So much so that it's deemed too impractical for most to consider ever doing. And not everyone is ready to go unmanaged. To flourish on your own, having patience and discipline is almost mandatory. You have no benchmarks for performance other than those you set for yourself.

Then how can a Millennial with an idea or passion make an impact if he or she has too much at stake, too much student loan debt to repay, or too many mouths to feed?

By doing it on the side and hustling inches closer every day.

HUSTLE AND GROW

I don't have a better example to share other than my own. I am a financial advisor who worked for other people before launching my own wealth management firm. At first glance, this may not seem like your classic tale of entrepreneurship: the American Dream you see on *Shark Tank*. But the careful steps I took to establish my own brand, while earning a stable income elsewhere, are translatable to anyone's career path. Here's how it happened.

Before I even graduated college, expectations were set for me. My father opened a satellite office of his financial planning practice in Gainesville, where I worked during school and would continue providing service afterward. He wanted this to be his succession plan and the ticket to his retirement someday. I learned much of what I know from him, no doubt.

But within that first year out of college, I knew our father-son team wasn't working out. As generous as his time and energy were, we disagreed about almost everything.

The day-to-day was growing too hard for our relationship to bear, and that wasn't even what kept me up at night. I was captivated by helping people with their finances, but I wanted more. I wasn't going to be happy with a lifetime of servicing my father's preexisting relationships. I wanted to help my own type of clients, on my own terms, and in my own firm. Oh, and I wanted to move to New York City to do it.

When I told him, honestly, I think he was heartbroken. But like the loving father that he is, he vowed he would not stand in the way of my dreams. He sent me up north with a hug and my two duffel bags, more uncertain than me about whether it would work out.

I was moving to one of the most expensive cities in the world. And no, my parents did not lend me a dime. I had a small cash reserve saved from living at home for a year (a decision I think there's no shame in making). Heather told me what it would cost to find a roommate in a decent apartment on Craigslist, and I used my cash flow analysis to understand how much I would need to earn to get by. I mean really, *just get by*—I made meals for a whole week from two pounds of ground beef chuck (and was proud of myself already)! Without being a master of cash flow, I never would have had the confidence to go all in.

After some interviews, I secured a position as an associate advisor in a Park Avenue practice. I wrote financial plans and performed administrative work to help my boss's business run smoothly. In addition to my base salary, I negotiated a subsidy for my continuing education—I wanted to become one of the youngest Certified Financial Planners in the country. This would help legitimize me in a field where most successful professionals were much older. I worked like a dog servicing clients, studying, and starting to figure out how I'd find clients of my own. The goal would be to phase out my base salary for client revenue. But it became clear very fast that this wasn't going to be achieved through cold calling. I needed to be patient, keep my head down, and learn.

If you are fortunate enough to work in the industry you'd like to spin off in, that's great. Even under the thumb of someone else, you are gaining on-the-job training that applies to your craft. You might be in for a long game, but again, you need to be patient. This is the most practical way to fulfill your financial obligations while getting closer to your goal. You can see what works and what doesn't—and it's not your butt on the line. Witnessing someone else's business decisions (even when they're wrong) can teach you valuable lessons you will have forever.

If your dreams are a complete pivot from your current career, consider this: *time is your best friend.* You want to be working a job that maximizes your work-life balance. Then you can invest your free time into that entrepreneurial venture. This doesn't necessarily mean that you up and leave your full-time job to become an Uber driver. It doesn't have to be that dramatic of a shift. There might be ways to stick it out in your current industry, but in a more limited capacity or role. You can reclaim time in your life with simple changes. You just need to look for them.

Anyway, you read earlier about what happened to Heather during the Recession, but you didn't hear my side of the story. Within days of my arrival to the Big Apple, the bottom fell out. The last person you wanted to be was a financial professional, as I fielded no less than a dozen hysterical phone calls per week from my boss's clients claiming the sky was falling. But dealing with them was the easier part of my day.

Through the following years, I watched Heather and our peers struggle, terrified that the decisions they made were the wrong ones, not knowing how they'd ever start their careers or have the chance to do what they knew they were capable of. Heather was (and is) an incredibly strong woman and she felt like a victim. That was what killed me. No one so strong should feel incapable of improving her situation, no matter how bleak.

I realized that my real goal wasn't just to be my own boss, but to educate and empower Millennials. Older financial advisors were dismissing my generation as the entitled children of their clients. They had no idea how to assist with the new challenges we faced breaking into the workforce, or how to answer our unique financial questions regarding student loan debt repayment. More importantly, there were no wealth management firms run by Millennials for Millennials. With retirements of their own to worry

about, older advisors weren't willing to invest in people just starting their careers with challenges they
couldn't relate to. I could relate to them because I was
living them. There was a crack in my industry and I
hoped to be one of the first to fix it.

As the economy recovered, I switched firms and
recouped some time to start brainstorming my plan
of action. Although I had made some friends living
in the city, I knew I would need a bigger network to
grow a business, as mine wasn't large enough to form
a meaningful pipeline for new clients. Attending a re-
nowned business school program would expand my
network and enhance my credentials; two gains for
the price of, uh, a vacation condominium?

Before deciding to enroll, I carefully considered
what would need to occur to make a return on my
investment. Indeed, the cost was exorbitant, and I
just watched Heather learn the hard way about making uninformed financial decisions with her student
loans. I decided that the only way it would make sense
to pursue my MBA would be in a night program, so
that I could borrow less money and continue to make
money during the day.

But wait, you might ask, didn't he warn us earlier about the perils of pursuing graduate degrees?
Are they worth it if not "required" to enter a certain
field? The takeaway here isn't that attending business
school will unlock the secrets for running a successful
business. Many successful entrepreneurs would argue
that no school can teach you entrepreneurship, and
that real mastery comes more from *doing* more than

anything else. In this limited context, business school happened to be my investment—an investment in my time and money to build the network and credentials I needed.

There will come a time when you need to make an initial investment in your business venture. It could be additional training, a piece of equipment, or straight up cash. From a numbers standpoint, give this investment as much attention as any other decision we analyze in this book. But be a little cavalier about the unknown. Every entrepreneur should possess a bit of bravery. It's why we are drawn to set out this way in the first place.

In pursuing my MBA, I formed relationships and even learned a thing or two about business. My expanding network of young professionals translated to new clients and referrals, many of whom were also friends. It felt so wonderful to root for them as they did for me. My investment was starting to pay off.

Right before I walked across the graduation stage at Radio City Music Hall, I took the plunge: I eliminated my base salary and started relying on only my clients to generate income. Heather and I got married in the fall before then, and her job provided us with the financial security and health benefits we would need to leave my salaried days behind. Her stability made it possible for me to get closer to my goal. The ebb and flow of our relationship allowed this to be my time. We were both okay with that, and if you are in a committed relationship, your spouse needs to be, too. (You will learn more about this in Chapter 7.)

From then, I went all in, setting out to prove that financial advice for Millennials wasn't a "niche"—it was the future. I sought the attention of national news organizations to become an authority on the subject and build a constant stream of press. Social media and technology helped me distribute educational content to the right people. I established relationships with nonprofit organizations and took leadership positions to affect the industry. Most importantly, I committed myself to providing outstanding service to my clients of all ages.

By December 2016, I was ready to go all in for real. I left my former organization to build my own firm, Bone Fide Wealth.

It took eight years from the day I hugged my dad goodbye in South Florida to make it happen. Eight years of training, education, patience, hustle, negotiation, compromise, success, and failure. And this is only the beginning. I'll say it again: nothing worth doing is easy. I keep this in mind with every challenge I face.

Millennials are doers, and we are doing more than ever. Our hunger to have an impact, create, innovate, and disrupt the status quo makes us natural entrepreneurs. Pair this spirit with a solid foundation in personal finance, and you can achieve this Great Thing in Life. You can be unstoppable.

Earning the Right to Invest

People think investments make them rich. That's why they love them; why Jim Cramer can scream at millions of viewers on television almost every day; why moviegoers clamor over *The Wolf of Wall Street* and *The Big Short*, despite their portrayal of how awful investments can be when manipulated for greed; and why Amazon once had 123,984 search results in its books department for that one single word: investments. It's about the glamour, the risk, and the *sizzle* when you get them right—and the things you can buy when you do.

Okay, okay, that's enough. Time to cool off.

I may sound like a grandpa to my young clients, calling in with their first load of cash looking to triple their earnings. But I don't care. Investments make up just one area of personal finance. And like we discussed earlier, you need to earn the right to invest by first prioritizing your goals, mastering your cash flow, and establishing the safety net of a cash reserve that's appropriate in size to where you are in life. If you've followed along and met those benchmarks, then we can talk about investments.

Investing tests the relationship between risk and reward. People invest to grow their money at a faster rate than placing it in the bank. Some consider it "putting your money to work."

This means that if you are willing to risk losing money by committing it to something that *could* generate income or profit, you *might* be rewarded for that risk in the form of greater income or profit.

But again, stay cool here. I know the concept seems sexy, but my goal for this chapter is to keep things simple and vanilla. We're going to stick to learning about stocks and bonds and discuss two very popular ways of investing in them. My colleagues might think I've lost my mind by simplifying things this much, but I can assure you this is what you need right now. No more than this.

STOCKS, BONDS, AND EVERYTHING IN BETWEEN

This type of investing involves the *capital markets*. Capital markets are financial markets, such as the stock market. This is where you buy and sell *securities*, which are financial instruments that represent ownership in companies, called *stock*, or the debt of companies, called *bonds*. While you're learning terminology, another word for stock is *equity* and another word for debt is *fixed-income*, but I will stick to using stocks and bonds from here on out.

There are other capital markets beyond ones for buying and selling stocks and bonds. You can practically find a market to invest in just about anything. There are markets that let you invest in commodities, such as oil and corn, or markets that let you invest in how *other* markets will do in the future.

Clearly, there's no shortage of investment products, and new ones are being manufactured every day. They range from simple and straightforward to terribly confusing. With so many options to choose, how does one even begin? Again, let's keep it simple. There are stocks, there are bonds, and then there's everything in between.

Owning stock of a company means you own a part of that company. You buy stock in units called *shares*, which are traded on exchanges, such as the New York Stock Exchange. Therefore, owning shares of stock entitle you to a portion of that company's value and profits. If a company does well, the value of its shares (or the income you receive from those shares) should increase. However, if a company does poorly, the opposite holds true. Stocks are viewed as risky investments because no company is immune to the chance of going out of business. Blockbuster Video, for example, didn't see the streaming video services industry coming nearly as fast as it did. Thus, it went the way of the Dodo. But just how risky a company is comes down to a number of factors, including strategic risk, compliance risk, financial risk, operational risk, and reputational risk, positioned around its ability to turn a profit and grow that profit today and in the future.

Let's view the relative risk of stocks by examining two companies: Tesla Inc. and The Coca-Cola Company. Automobiles that use alternative energy are harder to sell than soda. Therefore, investing in Coca-Cola is less risky than investing in Tesla. This is oversimplified, but a fact. We can all agree that Coca-Cola isn't going anywhere anytime soon, whereas it's uncertain if Tesla will survive the next decade. As of 2016, the company had just turned its first profit. Sure, there's no guarantee that Coca-Cola is going to be around forever either, but since 1886, it has survived and grown steadily. However, because of the perceived difference in risk, Tesla might offer a greater reward than Coca-Cola, should Elon Musk's vision break through to the mainstream car and energy industries.

Bonds are less risky than stocks. They are the equivalent of giving a personal loan to a company. The company you give your money to is then responsible for paying you interest on that loan, called a *coupon*, and returning your money, called your *principal*, when the loan is due. Bonds are considered less risky than stocks because the income is more predictable. Also, if a company goes bankrupt, bondholders are the first investors to be paid out from what's left, giving them priority over other investors like stockholders. However, like stocks, bonds come in many varieties, each offering different levels of risk and reward.

Let's view the bonds of two companies: General Electric (GE) and Netflix. Owning a General Electric bond is less risky than owning a Netflix bond. GE is one of the largest companies in the world, and its presence is pervasive throughout our economic system. It's literally one of the companies that are too big to fail. The likelihood of GE being unable to make its bond payments is extremely low, given a myriad of factors such as its rating, size, and overall financial health. Netflix has boldly changed the way we watch television and entertainment. Though it appears it's here to stay, it's not too big to fail. Therefore, assuming you are investing in bonds of similar quality respectively, it should be the riskier of the two. And you should not be too surprised to find out that the Netflix bond pays a higher coupon. There's that risk for reward relationship once more.

So, if you are going to invest, how do you know which stocks and which bonds to invest in? Well, if I knew which ones were going to be the big winners, would I tell you? Probably not! I'd keep those secrets to myself and make tons of money in the process. I also wouldn't be writing this book, but alas, here we are.

The bottom line is that it's impossible to pick the right investments on a consistent basis. People and professionals might tell you they can, but they are full of it. History proves that even Wall Street's best investment managers do a bad job picking only winners on a consistent basis.

(They probably would prefer you didn't know that.)

Because you can't predict how any individual stock, bond, or investment will perform, you must be diversified. This means you shouldn't invest all your money in one stock or bond. I am sure you've heard of the expression, "Don't put all of your eggs in one basket!" You want to spread the risk you're willing to take across a broad range of investments, so that if a few do poorly, you have others that might do better.

Mutual Funds and Exchange-Traded Funds

Rather than having to choose among thousands of stocks or bonds on your own, the financial industry has done you a favor. They created investment products that do this for you called *funds*. Funds are the most popular way for people to invest.

The two most popular types of funds are *mutual funds* and *exchange-traded funds* (ETFs). These products are created by financial institutions and can be considered "baskets" of individual stocks, bonds, or a combination of both. Funds can invest in hundreds to thousands of individual stocks and bonds, therefore making them an easy way to achieve diversification without having to pick and choose individual investments on your own. They also allow greater access to investing for people who don't necessarily have a lot of money to invest.

There are thousands upon thousands of mutual funds and ETFs to choose from, each with its own investment objective. For example, if you wanted to invest in only domestic companies of a certain size (such as large companies worth more than $100 billion), there's a fund for that. You could also just as easily buy a fund that invests in only small European companies, and so on and so on.

Mutual funds have been around for a long time—since 1924 to be exact. They remain the most popular way to invest, second to none. Mutual funds essentially work like this: you, the investor, buy shares of a mutual fund with a certain investment objective. That money is then pooled with other investors just like you.

Then, the pooled money is invested in one of two ways. The first way is by a fund manager, who is going to actively buy and sell investments that fall into the scope of the fund's objective with the goal of earning a return for the fund's investors. This is called *active management*. Remember that. The second way is called *passive management*. Instead of being actively managed, passive mutual funds will invest according to a predefined list of investments, called an *index*. Indices are predefined and meant to be representations of specific markets, such as the U.S. stock or U.S. bond market.

The S&P 500, for example, is one of the most popular indices, representing the 500 largest domestic companies. Although it does not represent all U.S. companies, it serves as a pretty good representation of the U.S. stock market and is commonly used as such.

I bet you're wondering which management technique is better. Active and passive mutual funds have their advantages and disadvantages, and it's a question that's debated frequently today. However, I can share with you that, lately, more money on average has been going into passively managed investments because of their lower cost, and active managers often struggle to do better than their benchmarks through long periods of time. According to U.S. market data released from Morningstar, Inc., in June of 2016,

$21.7 billion dollars flowed out of actively managed U.S. stock funds alone! This is why a relatively new type of fund, the exchange-traded fund (ETF), was created in the 90s. In a nutshell, an ETF is meant to replicate or track a particular index and provide you with a benchmark-like return at minimal cost. It's essentially the equivalent of a passively managed mutual fund, but with one main difference. Unlike mutual funds, ETFs are bought and sold just like stocks, which trade throughout the day on exchanges. Mutual funds, meanwhile, trade at the end of the day. This means that when you buy an ETF, you can get in and get out the investment more quickly than you could with a mutual fund, which is an advantage for many investors.

ETFs have some additional advantages, like lower minimum investment requirements and tax efficiencies. But typically, lower costs and the ability to get in and out are the features investors value the most. So, ETFs over index funds, right? Not necessarily. The answer requires a greater understanding of how you invest.

How Do I Invest?

As I explained earlier, you must first *earn* the right to invest. If you have not yet identified and prioritized your goals, mastered cash flow, and started working on a cash reserve, you simply aren't ready. But let's assume you are.

When you invest, you invest toward your goals. Lucky for you, you've already identified them. By having also quantified your goals, you know how much time you have on your hands to achieve them, which is critical when it comes to investing your money.

The rule of thumb here is that the longer timeframe that you have to achieve a particular goal, the more risk you can tolerate to get there. Why? Having more time allows you to make up for losses along the way. If you adopt this disciplined investing principle, then you might feel just as comfortable in the years that you lose money as you do in the years that you earn a return.

Let's look at an extreme example. It's early 2008, and you invested 100 percent of your retirement money in the S&P 500—all stocks. By March of 2009, you would have lost something like half of your investment. Losing this much of your investment is devastating (after all, the Recession *was* devastating). But, if you kept your investment where it was and made no changes to it, you would be pretty close to where you started in early 2008 by early 2010. Because retirement is a long-term goal, maybe more than 30 years away, you have the time to recover losses, even when they are catastrophic. However, I must note that as you become closer to achieving your goal, you should not be willing to take on as much risk.

Therefore, the second key point to investing is understanding your tolerance for risk. It's a subjective and emotional thing. You must reconcile your feelings about the crucial relationship between risk and reward—just like with selecting a college or grad school earlier. In the context of investing, though, it means that if you aren't willing to risk anything, you might not get the reward—or return—to achieve your goal in the time you wish. But that might be okay with you, too.

For example, let's assume that losing half of your money is enough to make you curl up naked in the fetal position on the floor. What does this say about your tolerance for risk? Well, it gives me a better understanding of how you feel in extreme situations like the Great Recession, from which I could infer how you would handle fluctuations large and small. In other words, how would you feel about losing 5 percent of your money in the "stock market"? How about 10 or 20 percent? This exercise, though very general, can help you understand your own tolerance for risk and then apply that tolerance to a particular goal's time horizon.

Once you know your investment time horizon and your tolerance for risk, you can start to think about how to allocate your money. This process is called *asset allocation*, which helps an investor understand how much of an investment should be placed in stocks and how much should be placed in bonds.

The process goes even further by demonstrating the specific types of stocks and bonds to invest in, called *asset classes*. Stocks are considered an asset class by itself, but it can be broken down even more. For example, within stocks, you can invest in U.S.

companies of varying sizes such as small, mid-size, or large U.S. company stocks.

Asset allocation is interesting stuff because it examines how to maximize reward by using different types of assets and by also taking into account an investor's particular tolerance for risk. Unfortunately, it gets very technical pretty fast, but there is a method to assist you.

The financial services industry did a good job categorizing general asset allocations by standardized tolerances for risk. These tolerances can be described as follows:

Aggressive

Moderately Aggressive

Moderate

Moderately Conservative

Conservative

Each of these categories has an approximate ratio of stocks to bonds. It can, very broadly, look something like this:

Aggressive	80–100% Stocks/0–20% Bonds
Moderately Aggressive	60–80% Stocks/20–40% Bonds
Moderate	40–60% Stocks/40–60% Bonds
Moderately Conservative	20–40% Stocks/60–80% Bonds
Conservative	0–20% Stocks/80–100% Bonds

Try not to be too bummed-out here, but I cannot lay out for you a detailed asset allocation, let alone tell you what funds to specifically invest in. First, my compliance office would murder me for making specific investment recommendations in a book. It's basically a cardinal sin! And not for nothing; each of you are individuals. There is no standard approach to creating a detailed asset allocation model. Again, if there was a specific investment selection process to adhere to, we'd all be rich.

I can, however, tell you that once you have an idea of what your broad asset allocation is for a given investment goal, you can start to choose which specific funds fit the allocation and build an *investment portfolio.* You can start your search for individual investments by looking for funds that are literally named with the investment objective you might be looking for.

For example, if your investment time horizon is long-term, and you've chosen to invest aggressively, you might want to look for funds with names containing "aggressive growth," "total market," or "total equity." But let me be very clear: I am not telling you to invest in something based on name alone. I am merely suggesting that you begin your search this way.

Once you've identified an investment that you think makes sense, you will need to do your homework; at the very least, locate and study that particular fund's fact sheet. These are typically found on the Website of the company managing the fund. The fact sheet is a great way to learn about the most pertinent fund information, such as its objective, top investment holdings, risk profile and characteristics, past performance, purchase information, and associated costs.

One of the most important considerations when investing in a fund or any investment is that last one: costs. I personally believe that investments, especially investments in funds, have become increasingly commoditized during that last 10 to 20 years. This means that there's not much difference between funds with similar objectives, and the main thing the fund companies are competing over are costs. I believe this will continue to happen more and more through the next decade as passive investment products (index funds and ETFs) become more popular than their actively managed counterparts.

Let's review the various costs associated with investing in funds. The following represents the main categories of expenses you will encounter:

Investment Expense or **Expense Ratio:** The annual cost of owning a particular investment or fund. It can be as small as a few hundredths of a percent, called basis points, to as high as 2 to 3 percent of the value of the fund. The investment expense is accounted for in your return of the fund. So, when discussing the performance of a mutual fund or ETF, we are always talking about performance after, or "net" of, this expense.

Investment Management Fee: The annual cost of having your portfolio invested by an investment professional or program, such as a financial advisor, investment platform, or "robo-advisor." The investment professional or program gets paid this recurring fee in exchange for constructing, monitoring, and maintaining your investment portfolio. This fee may or may not cover other investment-related expenses, such as trading costs and various account fees. Humans typically charge one percent of the portfolio's value, and the robots charge 0.35 to 0.50 percent.

Commissions: The per-transaction cost of having your portfolio invested by a professional. Every time a professional sells or purchases an investment for you, you will pay a fee. Commissions vary greatly depending on the investment product being sold. It's kind of antiquated to work with a professional in this regard. You might consider paying a blanket investment management fee instead.

Trading Fees: These fees come along with the actual purchase or sale of a particular investment or fund. They could exist when either investing on your own or with an investment professional. These fees are typically a fixed charge up to a certain purchase or sale amount, and they increase incrementally the more you buy or sell. These could be on top of any investment management fees or commissions.

No matter how you go about investing, it's critical that you are aware of what you are paying for because costs have a direct impact on your returns. And they can be controlled, for the most part, if you understand them well. For example, you can minimize costs like investment expenses and trading fees by choosing passive investments over active investments or limiting the frequency in which you buy and sell. Other costs, like investment management fees, could be eliminated entirely if you invest on your own.

DIY? TMI.

Let's last touch on the differences between investing on your own and investing with a professional. I make a living helping individuals invest toward their goals. Most of my clients trust my firm to manage their money in a way that puts their interests above everything else. But I'm not going to tell you that you can't do this yourself. Of course you can. Many people do, and they are going to save money doing so. You can take the lessons in this chapter, along with an unlimited number of online resources (Investopedia.com is my favorite) and execute an investment strategy that works.

But in my experience, I can tell you that most of my clients are too busy working toward their goals to do as good of a job as my firm can do for them. Their time is too valuable and too precious to be spent perfecting an asset allocation model or mulling through the tens of thousands of funds that exist to create the optimal investment portfolio. They find value in working with a professional to help them make the best decisions, because they can reinvest that time into work or their personal lives. What it comes down to is, what is your time worth to you?

CHAPTER SEVEN

WHEN TWO BECOME ONE...
AND THEN THREE

Heather and I had not traveled much together before our honeymoon in Italy. Between our lack of cash in college and her lack of time early in her career, the notion of taking off overseas seemed impossible. Which is probably why we spent more time planning our 12-day, four-stop tour rather than the finer details of the wedding itself.

We began by strolling Florence's cobblestone streets, sampling blue "puffo" gelato (it allegedly means Smurf) and stuffing our suitcases with leather goods and market cheese. We then indulged at a remote resort on the Tuscan Coast. During our day excursion to Giglio Island, Heather ate a bad clam that turned her into a barf-spewing dragon. There wasn't a corner drug store in sight, so I bought her a pack of cigarettes and told her to get smoking (something she would never, *ever* do). But even that couldn't calm the waters inside of her!

That night, she insisted I go to our romantic cliffside dinner reservation. Staring out into the darkness of the sea, my table lit only by candles, it kind of felt like she was dead, like I was a widower returning to this magical place to remember her. In hindsight, it was probably the entire bottle of red wine talking, but man, was I emotional. Back in our hotel room, I tearfully confessed my love to this barf-spewing dragon. "How could I live this life without you?" She cracked a smile for the first time all night.

Thankfully, the clam worked its way through. She was back in action by our arrival to the Amalfi Coast, just in time for cooking class in Ravello and music on the rocks in Positano. Sipping cold Peronis at a beachside café, we realized we were sitting beside another newlywed couple. They weren't feeling quite as carefree.

"You should've at least told me about the credit cards."

"Why? It's my money—my problem."

"We spent *a ton* of money on the wedding!"

"So?"

"Well, you know I have student loans. I thought we were going to combine our accounts!"

"Why would we do that?"

"Because we're *married?!* That's what married people do!"

Eavesdropping on other people's drama isn't our idea of a chill afternoon, but given my profession and our next round of drinks, we couldn't help it. This couple was supposed to be relishing in the happiest time of their lives, like we were! Even after the bad clam! Instead, they battled over the financial skeletons in their respective closets, floundering over how to pay off a wedding they couldn't afford.

Talk about a mood killer.

For the sake of completeness, I'll let you know that we finished our trip in Rome, touring the sites on the back of a golf cart. It was very gluttonous after a week-and-a-half-long carbo-load, but fitting for the ancient city.

Some might read this and wonder why we, a couple with six figures of student debt, would take such an extravagant honeymoon. (I have a feeling our parents were thinking just that.) But you see, this trip *was* our Great Thing in Life, and we had prioritized and saved for it accordingly. By the time Heather and I got married, we had already wrapped our heads around our finances. We understood our assets, our liabilities, our cash flow, and our emotional and honest goals. We knew what they were to each of us individually and how they would change together.

Maybe the newlywed couple on the beach didn't view their marriage beyond the band, the bar, and a clever hashtag. It was an event in their respective lives, not the start of their life together. Maybe it's easier for Heather and me to grasp the concept because we've been in each other's lives since we were so young. But even for us, some of our feelings about what marriage meant to us didn't surface until we tied the knot, like how we would feel if we had to go on without each other.

The moral of this story is that marriage isn't about saving for a fancy wedding or honeymoon. If you've only thought that far, you've got a long way to go. This chapter will discuss sharing your financial goals, joining personal finances, and protecting the things that are most important to you with insurance and basic estate planning.

THE GREAT MERGE

Many of my young clients view a beautiful wedding as a serious financial goal. And it might be—it's a massive financial marker in your lives. Though you'll obviously need to make sure you don't sit your college roommate with his ex-girlfriend, what you really need to focus on is how this merging of the minds, bodies, and souls affects your finances. Because as many of my elders have told me, what's mine is Heather's and what's Heather's is also Heather's.

Just kidding. Kind of. Not really.

Now, before teaching the concepts you've already mastered to your future spouse, you must revisit emotional honesty. And if you thought being emotionally honest with *yourself* was hard, try being completely honest with the person you love.

This is the time to have some very serious conversations about the goals you want to achieve together. Things such as whether you want to have children, where you want to live, whether you want to live religious lives (and to what extent), when you'd like to buy a home, how comfortable of a lifestyle you want to live, and so on. Some of these are must-haves, dealbreakers, for sure. But I can't tell you what should be most important to you. Let your mother guilt you about that.

Look, when you begin these conversations, there's a good chance that you're going to learn that you share similar goals and time horizons, making common ground easy to find. After all, you are each other's better halves, so it's no surprise that similar thinking brought you together in the first place. In other instances, you may discover differences or things you never knew about your partner, which are going to make for some pretty interesting talks. They might test your relationship, stir your emotions, and drain your energy.

Just keep in mind that friction is normal. Millennials are people with convictions and opinions about the future. We don't just roll over and disappear into our spouses, nor should we. But we do need to make room for someone else to hustle and shine by our sides. Being a quality lifelong partner requires you to persevere and compromise, shine bright and dim it down. For better or worse, once you're married, your triumphs and tribulations can't always be the star of the show.

Okay, enough with this kind of advice—I'm not Dr. Phil.

Because you are in it together, you should join financial forces and combine everything into the "family pot," right? Eh, it depends. Before you undergo the largest financial merger of your life, you should discuss the ins and outs of your finances with your partner, just like you discussed your joint financial goals. Like the couple on our honeymoon, so many people hide details from their spouses. This is absolutely, undoubtedly, 100 percent stupid—a one-way ticket to marital Armageddon. To be financially empowered as a couple, you must be transparent. If you're willing to share the bathroom, I think you can share your numbers, no matter how great or terrible they seem.

To get on the same page financially, you will disclose your respective incomes, expenses, assets, liabilities, benefits, and policies. That should cover the financial items needed to have constructive conversations about your whole picture. I recognize that there are certain financial items that might need to remain private, but these are the exception to the general rule that you must put as much information on the table as possible to make meaningful plans. Don't be private for the privacy's sake.

For example, as you know from earlier, Heather has an ass-ton of student loan debt, and I have some, too. But from the jump, we laid it out there. We decided to treat everything as one pile belonging to us both, just like our incomes. For me, it didn't matter that she had more debt. All I cared about was that we both were doing everything we could. It didn't take long for Heather to agree that we were in it together, and that it would take our collective efforts to succeed.

Don't take that as sugar coating reality, though. Even with years to come to terms with our joint situation, we still get into who spent what and who made what mistakes all the time. But the result is always, *who cares?* The only thing that makes mistakes of the past worse is secrets today. Transparency, kids. That's the key.

Once you've shared your financial lives with one another, you are going to need an appropriate structure in place. This means you will need to master cash flow together as a unit, and determine how you want to share checking, savings, and investment accounts, if any.

For cash flow, you can literally combine budgets. If you both are masters of cash flow, this won't be too hard. But if one person isn't as savvy, the more organized spouse will need to help build up his or her cash flow skills. A rogue spending partner is bad for your relationship and ultimate financial goals. Remember, it takes time—and now trust—to master cash flow, so be patient if you are dealing with someone less knowledgeable. Also, be sure to alter your joint budget for taxes because the taxes on your income change slightly after you get married.

Sharing accounts and debts is where things get sticky. Putting money in a joint account truly means that these assets are split 50/50 between partners. When Heather's year-end bonus was deposited into our joint account, she didn't like my joke about how her hard-earned bonus was now half mine. Of course, hers was a normal emotional reaction, but it illustrates my point. You and your partner's feelings may differ regarding who owns what because one partner earns more than the other, carries more debt than the other, or because one partner had brought existing assets into the marriage. You need to explore these feelings and talk them through. I can't tell you how to divide your financial life, but I can tell you that you both need to agree on an arrangement that makes everyone feel good.

As I mentioned, Heather and I chose to combine almost all our assets (and debts) together. Thus, it really didn't matter if she had earned a bonus or if I had a big month of production. It was all ours, regardless of how disproportionate our dollars were. Given our respective earning power, we knew that we would each have stretches of good years and less good years. Our careers are cyclical, and it took us years to build the confidence to get here. But we believe in our joint unit enough to know that we can trust and lean on each other financially now and in the future. You may or may not feel that way about your partner. Either way, that's okay. Let those feelings dictate what you ultimately decide to do.

Things are a little different in "community property" states. Property that is owned by one spouse before the marriage is sometimes referred to as the "separate property" of that spouse, but there are instances where the community can gain an interest in separate property and even situations where separate property can be "transmuted" into community property. The rules for this vary from place to place. To make things easy, let's assume you two are also subscribing to the "what's mine is yours" mentality. I recommend that you deposit all sources of income into a joint checking account. This is the account that you will use to pay your fixed and variable expenses each month such as rent, credit cards, and student loans. I believe that doing it this way creates fairness and transparency between partners. It also helps you stick to your budget and more easily identify savings to allocate toward your financial goals. For the hustling entrepreneurs or independently employed, you will want to deposit your withholdings for taxes in a separate savings account. Those monies should not be comingled with the money deposited in your joint account because they will need to be paid to the U.S. Treasury on a quarterly basis.

Speaking of savings, it is usually a great idea to systematically move those cash savings from your checking account to an appropriate savings account. You don't need a separate savings account for each of your cash-related savings goals (such as a cash reserve or house fund), but if compartmentalizing each of your goals into different savings account helps, go for it. I just don't think it's worth paying extra account fees to do what one account can do.

Even after you've merged cash accounts, I still believe that each partner should hold onto his or her own individual checking and/or savings account. Having this not only maintains your sense of independence, but it also allows you to make purchases that fall outside of the regular monthly expenses. Some call it a play account or, in my house, a pushke (Yiddish for "a little container").

For example, if Heather wants to buy Hazel and me presents (let's say, a bowl of truffled mush for Hazel or something practical for me that I don't realize is a gift until I'm using it), without us knowing about it, she can use her individual account to make the purchase knowing that we won't know about it and that it won't affect that month's cash flow. These accounts can be replenished when there's a surplus in savings, but remember the goal is not to hoard too much cash there because that's money that could otherwise be used toward joint financial goals.

Let's not forget about investment accounts. These are the accounts that are linked to joint financial goals like financial independence, but that are not retirement accounts like your IRA or 401(k) (which cannot be held jointly, anyway). Investment accounts should also be held jointly between spouses. Because you first have to earn the right to invest, it could be some time before you have the ability to save in an investment-related account, including retirement accounts.

Valuing Life (Insurance)

When we discussed employer benefits, we punted the topic of life insurance to this chapter. And here we are, after one of the happiest times of your life, ready to talk about death. Good times!

You've reached the point where the topic of life insurance becomes relevant because you have someone other than you to worry about. Simply put, life insurance provides someone of your choosing, called the beneficiary, with a death benefit should you die.

It should not be too hard to imagine how things could change dramatically if you lose your partner. The emotional toll would be unrivaled, and the financial consequences could be catastrophic at a time when money is the last thing on your mind. In many cases, the loss of a partner means the loss of his or her income. Life insurance might not help with the emotional aspects of loss, but it most certainly can help with the financial.

One might ask, "How can you place a value on a person's life?" This is a complicated question with answers that will almost always be wrong to someone. That's why lawyers fight about it all the time in court after a person dies. However, for our purposes here, we are not examining the value of life after death. We are just looking at the economic impact that the loss of your partner would have on you and your family, and how to protect yourself against that loss.

Earlier in this chapter, I asked you to identify and quantify your goals so that they could be properly planned for. Then, when you committed to a serious relationship, you merged those goals with your partner. Now, you can use that information to figure out what you or your partner might need in the form of life insurance to be able to continue the pursuit of your financial goals. Yes, your plans might dramatically change should you lose your companion, but a lot of times they don't. More importantly, your financial obligations don't just disappear.

There are plenty of life insurance calculators out there that can help you understand what you need. I like the one at Lifehappens.org. Calculators like this consider some common variables to determine your personal needs, such as: expenses, outstanding debts, mortgages, the decedent's loss of income, college educations, investment rates of return, and a factor for inflation. Otherwise, you can work with a financial professional to help you determine the appropriate amount of insurance to purchase.

Once you have obtained a figure that represents your current life insurance need, you can shop around for coverage. There are a lot of options out there, but I am going to make your life very simple. I highly recommend you start by purchasing *term life insurance*. Term life insurance policies offer coverage for a set amount of years, called the *term*. The most common term periods are 10, 20, and 30 years.

They also have a set annual cost, which you might remember, is called the *premium*. As long as you pay your premiums, you are insured. So, if you die during the term, your beneficiary will receive the death benefit, tax-free. Term life insurance is as simple as it can get, and it is also going to be the cheapest form of life insurance coverage available. Term life insurance policies are a commodity, so depending on the carrier and its rating, most are priced competitively for pretty much the same thing. For the young and healthy, it can be very affordable. (The opposite of term life insurance is *permanent life insurance*, which instead of offering coverage for a set term provides coverage for your entire life. Permanent insurance comes in many forms, and it is typically more expensive than term insurance.)

To qualify for coverage, you need to go through a process called *underwriting*. This is where the insurance carrier assesses your *riskiness*. After all, if you die young, they may have to pay out some serious money. Underwriting requires you to complete an application that will ask for basic information, as well as detailed medical information, such as whether you're a smoker or if you have any relevant family history or conditions. Typically, there is also a medical examination, which will result in a medical professional visiting you to take blood, urine, and various metrics, such as your height and weight. They could also ask you some of the same questions that you already answered on the application. Additionally, the carrier may request your medical records from your doctors to further evaluate your health.

Sounds intense? It can be, but it's necessary to obtain meaningful coverage. When underwriting is finished, you will receive a decision from the insurance carrier letting you know if you are eligible for coverage and at what health rating. Having good or excellent health can result in significant savings on your premiums, whereas poor health or smoking can result in higher premiums (*much* higher if you're a smoker, so please, don't smoke!). By the way, before even filling out an application, you can receive quotes based on your choice of policy design, and then you will have some idea of what insurance is going to cost you.

When shopping around, I'd make sure to use a carrier that has strong convertibility privileges, meaning you can convert part or some of the policy to a permanent one if you ever wanted to without needing to go through underwriting again. I also like term policies that let you reduce the benefit amount in the future. As you get older, you typically will find your needs for insurance decrease, so it could be helpful to reduce your benefit, and therefore expenses, by reducing your policy's benefit amount. Again, working with a good financial advisor can help you understand all the aspects of life insurance.

Life insurance strategies beyond basic family protection are beyond the scope of this book, but what you've just learned will set you up to utilize other strategies later on. Just like we discussed with disability insurance earlier, the goal right now is to feel better about knowing that the financial risk of something awful happening is transferred mostly off your shoulders.

THE ESTATE PLANNING STARTER KIT

Heather and I got married in 2013, almost a decade after our first date. During those early years, we did some really stupid, irresponsible shit, both together and apart. None of it fazed us at the time; not even a blip on the radar. But after we got married, I noticed a change in the way she views risk, especially her fears for my general safety running around the streets of Manhattan. Clearly, we have different definitions of what the flashing red hand on the other side of the crosswalk means.

While I find her concerns more endearing than anything, the financial advisor in me automatically thinks of the documents that would protect her should I actually kick the bucket. I refer to them as the Estate Planning Starter Kit, which consists of the following critical components: a last will and testament, a financial durable power of attorney, a healthcare proxy, and a living will.

The most widely talked about estate planning document is the *last will and testament,* or will, for short. This document spells out who receives your possessions and assets when you die. However, it does more than explain where your "stuff" should go. It also states other important information, such as who you want to place in charge of administering your estate, and who you want the guardian(s) of any minor children to be, should you have any. It is important to note that without this document, your state government will be the one handling your affairs in accordance with state law, which is usually a less-than-ideal situation.

In addition to a will, your starter kit should have a *durable power of attorney*, which is responsible for assigning an individual, known as the "attorney in fact," who can make financial decisions for you if you become incapacitated. Therefore, should bills need paying, investments need managing, or assets need to be sold, this document will allow the attorney in fact to act on your behalf. Given the large amount of power and responsibility these powers can place on a person, it is usually a good idea to choose someone you trust.

The next component in your kit is a *healthcare proxy*. Much like a durable power of attorney, this document permits a specified person, the agent, to make medical decisions on your behalf, allowing them the ability to authorize medical procedures and treatments. Once again, choosing a trustworthy agent is critical. It may even make sense to have a conversation with the agent so that they clearly understand what your wishes are, heaven forbid the situation arises.

The final piece to your starter kit is a *living will*. This document outlines your wishes if you are not only incapacitated, but also if death is imminent, or if you are in a persistent vegetative state.

Due to their very nature, these areas of estate planning can be as serious as they are emotional.

Some clients have been fearful and panicked, just brushing the surface of them. However, it's important to recognize that, should the worst arise, the emotional cost is typically far worse than spending a few hours and dollars to put an estate plan in place.

As one last recommendation, I would stay away from online legal service Websites to build out your starter kit. Although I am all for technology making our lives easier, when it comes to matters as serious as these, it's best to work one-on-one with a trusted legal professional. So, get it done. And be careful crossing the street.

Just like having money is nothing without goals, getting married is nothing without commitment—a commitment to sharing the good and the bad with one another, to protect each other, and to celebrate the Great Things in Life when you experience them as a team. Even if a bad clam tries to get in the way.

Poppin' Bottles

Despite my profession, Heather is the planner in our crew. She is the one circulating lists thumbed on her iPhone and filling our weekends with activities. Having an agenda is her agenda. So, in early 2015, it was no surprise when she decided that we would be having a State of the Marriage Address.

She had questions that needed answers. Would we move apartments? Would we stay or leave the city? Would we travel? Would we have a baby? And when, *when, WHEN?* Rather than continue to fight about this rotating list of big questions, she proposed we set a date to talk about them all at once.

About a month later, over a bottle of wine, we made some major life decisions. We would continue to save money by remaining in our one-bedroom apartment on the Upper West Side; we would hit the pause button on surfing Zillow for homes outside the city; we would take some domestic trips, but nothing crazy; and we would stop trying to prevent having a baby.

Note the double negative on that last one. At that point in time, we couldn't fully admit to ourselves that we wanted to have a child. That would be too vulnerable, too uncertain. But we could concede that if we *happened* to get pregnant, we would *happen* to be happy about it.

We obviously had it all figured out. Obviously.

We didn't think there was a chance in hell it would happen that week. We conducted the State of the Marriage Address in South Florida, while we were in Miami for Heather's best friend's wedding. One night of bottomless mojitos and samba dancing later, she was unknowingly carrying the seed of our spawn.

Less than a month after the big talk, every piece of our well-discussed plan changed. We needed to find a bigger apartment in a more affordable neighborhood. Aside from a few short business trips, we wouldn't be traveling anywhere—too expensive. We would jump back on the house hunt after our new addition arrived, again pushing up our date to leave New York City.

We had nothing figured out. Nothing.

Getting pregnant was only the start of things we couldn't control. Hazel Shaine Boneparth, our little hazelnut, was born a whole month early at a teeny 5 pounds and 1 ounce. When we took her home from the hospital late on a Thursday evening, it was to an ill-prepared apartment of unopened boxes and un-washed bottles. We triaged the situation thanks to Heather's mom, the new grandma formerly known as Robin and now exclusively referred to as Rah Rah. And it's been a flurry of surprises ever since.

From when we first broke the news about Heather's pregnancy until now, it's been interesting how many uncomfortable conversations we've been sucked into about our friends' timelines for having kids of their own. I guess it was something about us taking the leap in our rat race of a city that makes people want to talk about it. Like they must justify to us why they too don't want to have kids right now, or when they think they'll be able to squeeze it in.

"He wants to make partner first."

"We are redoing the pool this year."

"We have too many Starwood points."

We've heard it all, and without ever asking, really. For someone who used to plan a week's worth of dinners on Sundays, Heather's response is always ironic but captivating: "There will never be a right time. You just have to be open and willing to accept change."

She's right. Expanding your family opens you to a world filled with question marks. Out of all the major life changes we've discussed in this book, it's the hardest one to control, because you can't. It's not just getting pregnant, birthing a healthy baby, figuring out child care, or arranging for education down the road. It's a lifetime of constant change. The whole point of this exercise, of finding solutions for Millennials, is not just to achieve the Great Things in Life, but to be equipped to sustain change. To embrace it and let it enrich your lives.

Next, we will consider altering cash flow for your family, child care expenses, and revisiting insurance and estate planning, if necessary.

When it came to kids, my Grandpa Sheppard always said: "Love finds a way." Years after he passed away, I now get where his was coming from. There's nothing Heather and I wouldn't sacrifice for Hazel. (Cue Creed's "My Sacrifice," which I hope is now stuck in your head. Gotcha!) But to be honest, I'd prefer not to sacrifice all that much. Grandpa Shep's adage is cute, but doesn't help us understand the more pragmatic side to having kids. Even though you can't plan for everything in this department, you can tinker with your cash flow to get a sense of how costs might change in your new world as parents.

Like all the other life changes, if you follow *The Millennial Money Fix* and become a master of cash flow, you will have an easier time figuring out the impact that a child will have on your expenses. There is plenty that you can figure out in advance, even just using estimates.

According to a 2015 U.S.D.A. report, the average middle-income family will spend approximately $12,650 on child-related expenses in their baby's first year.[1] That's an average. But people are literally *gaga* for babies, so you know the Internet is chock-full of resources to help you figure it out more. Babycenter.com is a great resource, and they have a very comprehensive First-Year Baby Costs Calculator that you can use to try to pinpoint your baby expenses.[2] At the least, it will provide you with a list of goods and services you might need. You can also use the site's Cost of Raising a Child Calculator, which is tad more straightforward.[3]

There are some significant initial expenses associated with having a child, otherwise known in our home as *baby swag*. You need furniture, clothes, strollers, car seats, and waterproof changing pads shaped like peanuts. Because of these big purchases, you need to not only work the expenses for the child into your cash flow, but you also need enough cash on hand to buy baby swag. If you managed to build a cash reserve, you should have no problem with this.

Before you go nuts buying baby Burberry, though, think back to our cash flow discussion regarding the lifestyle expenses in college. Remember that? If you can afford to dress your kid like Saint West, by all means start a Snapchat account and get posting. But keep in mind that the primary goal is to ensure your little one is happy and healthy. There are strollers that cost a thousand bucks and ones that cost a hundred. Aside from some tricked out wheels, they both will get the job done. Don't be so concerned with what everyone else is doing with their children. You just focus on doing everything you can for yours. And if you have the funds for a waterproof changing pad shaped like a peanut, buy it.

Interestingly, one cash-positive thing about having a baby is watching your personal spending habits change. For many Millennial couples, new baby expenses can balance out by a reduction in lifestyle expenses. Heather and I have noticed a substantial decrease in our monthly credit card bills since having a baby. We used to dine out, a lot. Heather even had a food blog dedicated to our grubbing around the city, but she went on semi-permanent hiatus when morning sickness put her on an all-bread diet for nine months. Now that we bought a house in Northern New Jersey, we find ourselves staying in even more because we are just pooped. Adding a commuter train ride to both ends of our workday makes it much harder to care for the Hazelnut, but much easier to spend less money. Even if Heather still insists on shopping at Whole Foods, pizza delivery is half-price in the 'burbs, so we're coming out on top.

We can't leave the baby cash management conversation without addressing one of the biggest expenses of all: child care. According to a 2015 Care.com report, the average weekly cost of a nanny for one child is $477 and $488 for two. The average weekly cost of a daycare facility is $188 for one child and $341 for the second.[4] These are just averages, as the costs in major metropolitan areas are much higher.

You can figure out what you can afford by plugging the projected cost into your cash flow. Especially in places where the cost would be a disproportionate chunk of the household income, you might realize that you need to try a more creative arrangement. In New York City, for example, full-time nannies can cost up to $900 per week, and many want to be paid in cash. That's your hard-earned, after-tax dollars right there. For couples with two working spouses, it might make sense for one partner to stay home during those first few years, or make a career pivot to something part-time or more flexible. You're going to have to run the numbers, factoring in items like losing employer benefits. Emotional honesty comes back into play too, as it's a bold move to put your career on hold to raise a child.

After Heather's three-month maternity leave ended, I spent two days working from home and caring for Hazel, and we hired a nanny for the other three days. It was an incredibly difficult feat, but it helped us continue to save the money we needed to close on (and furnish) our house. Looking back, I wouldn't trade those afternoons in Central Park with her for anything in the world.

Cost isn't the only reason child care is a sensitive subject. We're talking about someone, often a stranger, taking care of the most precious little person in your life. Yet, you have to implicitly trust them like family to function and keep earning the money you need to thrive. Heather feels like it's a double-edged sword. She wants to work, but needs help, but wishes she didn't need anyone's help at all.

To that point, don't take for granted the help of your family and loved ones. Our closest family is more than an hour drive away. We can't begin to express how much we appreciate when family visits and gives us a much-needed break. In the past, we'd go months without a visit—by our own choosing—and now, we'd like to see them every day if we could! And that's not just because we want to sit down at a restaurant like civilized adults. It's because trusting blood is easier than strangers, and because you look at your child the way that your parents look at you and the baby. Money can't buy those feelings. If you can find a way to incorporate your family into your child care situation, even if it's at the expense of your comfort, I strongly suggest you do it. Have a spare bedroom? Offer it to Grandma and Grandpa, as often as they'll come.

Having a child will prompt some revisions to your protection planning needs. Before marriage, you assessed the importance of protecting your income so that if something knocked you out of commission, you could continue to pursue your financial goals, knowing that your earning power is protected as you mount your recovery. After marriage, you protected yourself with life insurance to ensure that your significant other could financially survive without you. Now, with a little goober at home, your need to protect your family is much more significant from an insurance standpoint.

In the case of disability insurance, if you didn't acquire some form of coverage already, now is the time to revisit fitting these policies into your family picture. If you disregarded life insurance previously, I encourage you now, more than ever, to consider obtaining it. If you're healthy, there's almost no excuse, given how affordable coverage can be. Even if you've already obtained coverage, you should probably still revisit the topic after starting a family to determine whether you must recalculate the amount you need.

As you know by now, my goal isn't to scare you into thinking that something awful will happen to you. Rather, my objective is to have you reevaluate the *risks* in your life given the increased *responsibility* in your life. I sleep better at night knowing that if anything happened to Heather or me, our family would be taken care of and able to move forward in the direction that we are working toward.

As you might have guessed, a second trip to the land of insurance also means another trip to the bright and bushy world of estate planning. Earlier, this chapter provided you with an understanding of the basic estate planning documents that you should have in place once you're married. You learned that there are documents that dictate who can make financial or medical decisions for you, as well as where your stuff goes when you die. But now that you have the most precious thing of all, a child, you are going to need to figure out where he or she goes if you and your partner are unable to care for them.

Just when you thought this topic couldn't get any gloomier, I done did this.

Seriously, imagine the conversation that most couples—including Heather and I—have had regarding guardianship, which becomes a part of your last will. I'm not about to spill the details of ours here because we'd still like to be speaking to our parents after they read this book. This is a seriously tough conversation to have, facing an unthinkably tough situation. Depending on your familial relationships, it can get even pricklier.

As hard as it might be, you need to put your emotions aside and think about what's going to be in your child's best interest. Factors to consider when choosing a guardian for your child include geography, the health of the prospective guardian, your child's schooling and friends, and many more. Yes, in a perfect world, all the grandparents, aunts, and uncles would love your children to pieces and take them in as their own, ensuring their growth as good human beings. But in reality, not every person or living situation is the right fit, no matter how much love exists.

Okay, time to shake all this death talk off. Think about all that you've accomplished to get here. You are only able to plan for rainy days because you've also planned for sunny ones. And you've got a lot of living left to do. Let's move on to what the rest of life looks like for us.

CHAPTER EIGHT

FINANCIAL INDEPENDENCE IS THE NEW RETIREMENT

Even with the creative strategies outlined in these pages, the story will not end the same way for Millennials as it did for our elders. But this shouldn't be all that surprising.

Retirement is defined as the time when work is optional because not working is affordable. Typically, people retire when the money they've saved and income they've secured is enough to cover their lifestyle. Because it's so capital intensive—meaning it takes a lot of money—retirement is often the hardest goal for a person to achieve.

In the past, retirement was not an elusive concept; it was a concrete and predictable milestone. My grandparents lived a classic retirement on the golf course in South Florida, where their biggest concern was whether the deli meat in the fridge had spoiled. They saved up by living within their means during their working years. They received Social Security benefits, and my grandpa had a pension for his time served in World War II. His battle was harder than anything I'll ever do, so I am by no means diminishing their hard work. But they had a simple roadmap and entitlements. We simply might not.

For Millennials, retirement will be much more difficult to achieve than it is for our parents and was for our grandparents. As the Millennial Problem pointed out, we carry more student debt than any other generation. Servicing this debt is significantly hindering our ability to save for our financial goals—especially retirement, because it has the longest time horizon and is most likely to be placed last on our priority list. And there's no shortage of debate about whether our generation will be able to participate in programs like Social Security, which might be a thing of the past by the time it matters to us.

Other entitlements, such as employer pensions, are also slipping away. Heather's former company froze its pension plan a couple of years ago, citing costs of operation as the primary reason for the decision. But employees knew it went beyond the dollars and cents. Reflecting the sentiment of the labor environment shift, her company's CEO spoke quite publicly about the notion of careers, stating that people shouldn't plan to have one there. Rather, they should utilize their time at the company to receive top-notch training and move on. It should be a stop on their journey rather than their final resting place.

Sure, the "lifers" were pissed, but how could Heather be? She's had many jobs. She made swift moves early in her career to generate the earning power needed to service her debt, and then later found a way to balance her income and quality of life in a way that works for her. She gets what her former CEO was aiming for. Nonessential management jobs were being eliminated, so reaching for the next level wasn't possible. And that was okay. Why should that company incentivize people to plop in a cubicle for the next 20 years when that doesn't reflect their business model, or the realities of today's workforce?

The question remains, if fewer jobs are "for life," so to speak, how do Millennials account for career volatility while trying to plan for a stable future? This is most unsolvable problem for Millennials yet. We don't know what retirement will look like for us because it's unclear whether government or employer-funded programs will exist in the coming decades, or what additional surprises may come our way.

Keeping this in mind, I'll take a crack at a framework that combines the traditional retirement planning model with a new way of thinking about our future.

First, let's examine a traditional retirement planning calculation. The goal of retirement planning is to determine the probability that you will be able to maintain a lifestyle, defined in today's dollars, for a specific length of time in the future. Here are the basic variables and assumptions that many retirement calculators use:

Time: at what age you want to retire and for how long.

Lifestyle: the type of lifestyle you'd like to live during retirement, using today's after-tax dollars.

Rate of Return: the return you can get on your retirement assets.

Inflation: how much the cost of your lifestyle will increase each year.

Retirement Assets: what you've currently saved for retirement.

Retirement Savings: how much you are planning to save for retirement each year.

Retirement Income: how much you can expect to receive from various income sources, such as pensions and Social Security.

Playing with these variables is really just a game of push and pull. For example, if you want to retire earlier but would like retirement to last for the same amount of years, your probability of success will be decrease (all else remaining equal). But if you choose to retire at an older age, your probability of success will increase. There's a positive effect on your retirement outcome by increasing your rate of return, retirement assets, savings, or income. There's a negative effect on your retirement outcome by increasing your lifestyle or because of inflation.

The relationship between these variables is commingled. When one of them changes, your retirement outcome changes for better or worse. Consider this a throwback to your lesson on goal priority, where funding one goal will affect your ability to fund another. Similarly, to make constructive decisions around retirement planning, you need to remember that changing just one of the variables above will affect the end result.

But again, using just a traditional retirement planning model will not give Millennials all the answers. There's no guarantee that historical rates of returns driving the models will continue to hold true in the future. Some of us could end up repaying our student debt forever, never ridding ourselves of our earlier financial decisions. If Social Security is reduced or eliminated, we face greater pressure on our need to save so that someday work is optional. There is also the real likelihood that science and medicine could push average life expectancies well beyond our 80s, creating a need for more financial resources to sustain our lifestyles.

Then how can Millennials really achieve success, when retirement, as our predecessors know it, may not exist?

We need to view it differently.

Chapter by chapter, we've planned for your quest to achieve the Great Things in Life, as you defined them. There's a good chance that by prioritizing your goals, you will experience some of those things in your 20s and 30s. But other things—such as honing your career ambitions and finding time to pursue passion projects that inspire you—might take longer. Those are the Great Things in Life that not only fulfill your soul, but can also fill your wallet.

If Millennials are unabashed creators and constant disrupters, our ultimate goal should be to achieve something greater than doing nothing.

Maybe our retirement is not retirement at all. Maybe it's called financial independence: the pinnacle of our ability to do what we want.

Every Monday morning, I walk off my train and I am eager to work. It's the definition of happiness to know I'm about to embark on a week's worth of solving the problems and sharing in the successes of my clients. But who's to say that feeling will last forever? I would certainly like to teach financial literacy and personal finance as a professor in a more formal setting. Maybe having more financial independence will give me the flexibility to pursue that instead of marketing for new business all the time. But by saying I love what I do and that it doesn't feel like work, I realize I am one of the few Millennials (not the many) who can say that right now.

My wife—the self-proclaimed Millennial Problem—must maintain a six-figure salary to service her six-figures of student loan debt. For now, it's a reality of the situation she created and the needs of our family. Yet, she was able to pivot out of private law practice to something still challenging and with more predictable working hours. She reclaimed time to spend with our little Hazelnut and to pursue her relationship with writing. She even put her personal projects aside to write this book with me, in hopes of teaching others to ask the questions she should have years ago.

Writing a book was one of her Great Things in Life, and the mistakes of her 20s couldn't stop her from achieving it. Through her own actions, she gets closer to financial independence every day.

The truth is that Millennials didn't borrow to depths below our bank accounts to be told what to do. We did it because even if it wasn't crystal clear just yet, we felt a purpose somewhere deep inside for something. If we are acting with intent, with knowledge and that purpose in mind, we are getting closer to freedom.

Throwing out the traditional definition of retirement is not a rationalization for our shortcomings, but like everything else, a true change in course. Our issues require a new set of answers that combine the best tools we have with a fresh outlook on success. It's about the freedom to do what we want to do, whether that's nothing at all or everything at once.

The choice should be ours, and now it will be.

NOTES

NOTES

Chapter 1

1. The New York Life Center for Retirement Income at the American College of Financial Services, Press Release on the RICP Retirement Income Literacy Survey, "Crash course needed: four out of five Americans fail when quizzed on how to make their nest eggs last," December 3, 2014, available online at: *http://theamericancollege.edu/ricp-retirement-income-survey/press-release.php.*

2. FINRA Investor Education Foundation, Financial Capability in the United States 2016, released July 2016, available online at: *www.usfinancialcapability.org.*

3. Council for Economic Education, Survey of the States, Economic and Personal Finance Education in Our Nation's Schools 2016, availble online at: *www.councilforeconed.org.*

4. "A look at the shocking student loan debt statistic for 2017," Student Loan Hero, available online at: *https://studentloanhero .com/student-loan-debt-statistics.*

5. *See* Project on Student Debt, reflecting numbers from 2004 through 2014, the Institute for College Access & Success, available online at: *http://ticas.org/posd/ map-state-data-2015.*

6. *See* "The Student Loan Landscape," *Liberty Street Economics*, The Federal Reserve Bank of New York, February 18, 2015, available online at: *http://libertystreeteconomics .newyorkfed.org/2015/02/the_student_loan-landscape.html#.VoWGCJMrIWK.*

7. Lend Edu, "Student Loan Debt Statistics 2017," July 1, 2016, available online at: *https://lendedu.com/blog/ student-loan-debt-statistics.*

8. Charles Lane, "How student loans help keep expensive schools in business," *Washington Post*, August 26, 2015, available online at:

https://washingtonpost.com/opinions/how-student-loans-help-keep-expensive-schools-in-business/2015/08/26/e7d7f83a-4c11-11e5-902f-39e9219e574b_story.html, citing Jason Delisle, "The Graduate Student Debt Review: The State of Graduate Student Borrowing," New America Education Policy Program, March 2014, available online at: *https://static.newamerica.org/attachments/750-the-graduate-student-debt-review/GrudStudentDebtReview-Delisle-Final.pdf*.

9. *See* Robert I. Lerman and Stefanie R. Schmidt, "An Overview of Economic, Social, and Demographic Trends Affecting the US Labor Market," The Urban Institute, Washington, D.C., Final Report (August 1999), *http://dol.gov*.

10. *See* United States Census Bureau 1997, 2002, 2007 and 2012 Economic Census.

11. Numbers drawn from the American Society of News Editors' annual newsroom diversity surveys, available online at: *http://asne.org/newsroom_census*.

12. For a lengthier discussion, read "A Less Gilded Future," *The Economist*, May 5, 2011, available online at *http://economist.com/node/18651114*.

13. United States Census Bureau Press Release, "Millennials Outnumber Baby Boomers and Are Far More Diverse, Census Bureau

Reports," June 25, 2015, available online at: *https://census.gov/newsroom/press-releases/2015/cb15-113.html. See also* Pew Research Center, "Millennials overtake Baby Boomers as America's largest generation," April 25, 2016, available online at: *http://pewresearch.org/fact-tank/2016/04/25/millennials-overtake-baby-boomers.*

14. Boston Capital Group Perspectives, "How Millennials Are Changing the Face of Marketing Forever," January 2014, available online at *https://bcgperspectives.com/content/articles/marketing_center_consumer_customer_insight_how_millennials_changing_marketing_forever.*

15. Ibid.

16. Housing contributes 15–18 percent of our gross domestic product. *See https://nahb.org/en/research/housing-economics/housings-economic-impact/housings-contribution-to-gross-domestic-product-gdp.aspx.*

Chapter 3

1. Pew Research Center, "The Rising Cost of *Not* Going to College," released February 11, 2014, available online at: *www.pewresearchcenter.org.*

2. Georgetown University McCourt School of Public Policy, "The Economic Value of College Majors," 2015, available online at:

https://cew.georgetown.edu/cew-reports/ valueofcollegemajors.

3. Average Public Undergrad Charges by Sector 2015–16, The College Board, available online at: *https://trends.collegeboard.org/college-pricing/figures-tables/average-published-undergraduate-charges-sector-2016-17.*

4. National Center for Education Statistics, Average graduate tuition and required fees in degree-granting postsecondary institutions…, 2014–2015, available online at *https://nces.ed.gov/programs/digest/d15/tables/ dt15_330.50.asp?current=yes.*

5. Steve Odland, "College Costs Are Out Of Control," *Forbes*, March 24, 2012, available online at *http://forbes. com/sites/steveodland/2012/03/24/ college-costs-are-soaring.*

6. *See* Paul F. Campos, "The Reason College Tuition Costs So Much," *New York Times*, April 4, 2015, available online at *http:// nytimes.com/2015/04/05/opinion/sunday/the-real-reason-college-tuition-costs-so-much .html?_r=0.*

7. The National Center for Education Statistics, Table 303.25, Total fall enrollment in degree-granting postsecondary institutions, by control and level of institution: 1970 through 2014, prepared October 2015 and available

online at: *https://nces.ed.gov/programs/digest/ d15/tables/dt15_303.25.asp?current=yes.*

8. Jordan Friedman, "10 Universities with the Most Undergraduate Students," *U.S. News & World Report*, September 22, 2016, available online at: *http://usnews.com/education/best-colleges/the-short-list-college/articles/2016-09-22/10-universities-with-the-most-undergraduate-students.*

9. President Barack Obama, "Remarks by the President on America's College Promise," The White House: Office of the Press Secretary, available online at: *https://obamawhitehouse.archives. gov/the-press-office/2015/01/09/ remarks-president-americas-college-promise.*

10. Governor Andrew Cuomo, "Governor Cuomo Presents 1st Proposal of 2017 State of the State: Making College Tuition-Free for New York's Middle Class Families," available online at: *https://governor.ny.gov/news/ governor-cuomo-presents-1st-proposal-2017-state-state-making-college-tuition-free-new-york-s.*

11. Learn more about the types of financial aid and how to apply on the U.S. Department of Education's Website for Federal Student Aid, *https://studentaid.ed.gov/sa.*

12. One useful database of available scholarships is through Peterson's, a Nelnet Company. *See http://petersons.com.*

Chapter 4

1. Visit the National Student Loan Data System, *https://nslds.ed.gov/nslds/nslds_SA.*

2. For a comprehensive overview and frequently asked questions about federal loan consolidation, visit *https://studentaid.ed.gov/ sa/repay-loans/consolidation.*

Chapter 5

1. At the time of publication, The Patient Protection and Affordable Care Act, otherwise known as Obamacare, was still in effect. The authors recognize that the state of publicly available healthcare may be in transition in 2017 and beyond. Stay tuned with rest of us.

2. For a complete list of definitions, you can visit *www.healthcare.gov/glossary.*

3. The authors do indeed have a friend who broke his arm doing a New Year's dance in New York City.

4. 457 plans rarely offer employer contributions.

Chapter 7

1. Mark Lino, Kevin Kuczynski, Nestor Rodriguez, and TusaRebecca Schap, "Expenditures on Children by Families, 2015," United Stated Department of Agriculture, available online at: *https://cnpp.usda.gov/sites/default/files/crc2015.pdf.*

2. View Babycenter.com's First-Year Baby Costs Calculator at *http://babycenter.com/baby-cost-calculator.*

3. View Babycenter.com's Cost of Raising a Child Calculator at *http://babycenter.com/cost-of-raising-child-calculator.*

4. *See* Source for the 2015 Cost of Care Infographic available online at: *https://care.com/c/stories/6811/sources-for-the-2015-cost-of-care-infographic.*

INDEX

INDEX

ABOUT THE AUTHORS

ABOUT THE AUTHORS

DOUGLAS A. BONEPARTH

Early in his career, Douglas A. Boneparth became one of the youngest CERTIFIED FINANCIAL PLANNER™ professionals in the country. In 2016, he was named to the InvstmentNews Top "40 Under 40." He serves as the CFP Board Ambassador for New York, educating the public about how financial planning with CFP® professionals can help people achieve their financial goals. There are only 50 certified financial planners honored with this distinction worldwide. He is the president and founder of Bone Fide Wealth, LLC, a Manhattan-based wealth management firm.

Douglas has helped his clients negotiate sales of businesses; establish legacies for future generations; purchase new homes; and pay off debt and achieve financial independence. While servicing the needs of his diverse book of business, he noticed a gaping hole in the industry: advice for Millennials, his peers. So while everyone else was chasing old money to invest, Douglas started finding young people to invest in.

To bring financial literacy and empowerment to Millennials, Douglas conducts seminars across New York City, including at the NYU School of Law, NYU Stern School of Business, and the New York City Bar Association. He is active in w!se, a New York City non-profit that teaches financial life skills to high school students.

Douglas is a leading media source on Millennial finance, appearing on CNBC's *On The Money* and *Nightly Business Report,* ABC's *World News Tonight* and *Good Morning America,* and Fox & Friends, and in *The New York Times* and *The Wall Street Journal,* among many others.

Douglas received his Bachelor of Science degree from the University of Florida and his Master of Business Administration from the NYU Stern School of Business, with concentrations in finance and management. He enjoys playing tennis and volleyball, keeping his menswear fresh and watching college football with Heather and Hazel, his wife and daughter.

HEATHER J. BONEPARTH

Raised as an only child (and grandchild), Heather Boneparth's father always said she was reared like veal—sheltered in close captivity to reach maximum potential. Breaking out of her box, she attended the University of Florida, where she earned her bachelor's degree, magna cum laude, in journalism. Through her studies, she traveled to Ecuador to report on indigenous life, wrote for local and national publications, and fell hard for writing.

As if journalism was not stressful enough for Heather, she abandoned her collegiate dreams and attended law school in New York City. Her legal thesis, assessing the media's liability for outrageous newsgathering techniques, was published in the fall of 2009 and has since been cited in federal court opinions and legal resources. A self-proclaimed dark horse, she never participated in class but wrote a mean final exam. She graduated with honors.

With two degrees and six figures of debt, Heather lawyered. And lawyered. In early 2013, she left the grip of private firm practice to pursue a more sustainable life in the insurance industry. Her side hustle was strong, and she rekindled her passions in the free time she gained back.

That is, until she and her husband Douglas learned they were expecting a baby girl. What better time to write a book about personal finance? While out on maternity leave, she spent her sleepless nights with Hazel in one arm and her laptop in the other. Helping Douglas market and manage his growing brand is rewarding, but writing this book is her Great Thing in Life: helping others from her own learned lessons, while doing what she loves.

The third annual "40 Under 40" project spotlights 40 dynamic honorees, all under age 40, who were selected from a pool of approximately 800 nominees by a panel of reporters, editors, and other representatives of InvestmentNews. Winners were chosen based on their level of accomplishment, contribution to the financial advice industry, leadership, and promise for the future. For more information visit *www.investmentnews.com*.